Egg Whites or Turnips?

Egg Whites or Turnips?

Archaeology and Bible Translation

Paul J. N. Lawrence

WIPF & STOCK · Eugene, Oregon

EGG WHITES OR TURNIPS?
Archaeology and Bible Translation

Wipf & Stock
An Imprint of Wipf and Stock Publishers
199 W. 8th Ave., Suite 3
Eugene, OR 97401

www.wipfandstock.com

PAPERBACK ISBN: 978-1-7252-6035-1
HARDCOVER ISBN: 978-1-7252-6034-4
EBOOK ISBN: 978-1-7252-6036-8

Manufactured in the U.S.A. 06/15/20

Contents

Acknowledgments *vii*

Abbreviations *ix*

1. Archaeology and Bible Translation **1**

2. "Is There Any Flavor in the White of an Egg?" Job 6:6 **15**
How Ancient Texts Have Shed Light on the Old Testament Text

3. "He [King Uzziah] Made Machines . . . to Shoot Arrows and Hurl Large Stones" 2 Chr 26:15 **22**
The Archaeology of Artifacts

4. "Praise Him with the Tambourine and Harp" Ps 149:3 **26**
The Archaeology of Music

5. "He [King Solomon] Described Plant Life, from the Cedar of Lebanon to the Hyssop That Grows Out of Walls" 1 Kgs 4:33a **38**
Translating Plants and Trees

6. "He [King Solomon] Also Taught about Animals and Birds" 1 Kgs 4:33b **58**
Translating Animals, Birds, and Other Creatures

7. "They Will Sparkle in His Land like Jewels in a Crown" Zech 9:16b **70**
Translating Precious Stones

8. "Unclean! Unclean!" Lev 13:45b 76
The Archaeology of Disease

9. "A Lion Shouted" Isa 21:8 79
How the Dead Sea Scrolls Help Us to Better Understand the Hebrew Bible

10. "Woe to Me That I Dwell in Meshek" Ps 120:5 82
The Archaeology of Places

11. "Faith Is the Title Deed of Things Hoped For" Heb 11:1 95
The Archaeology of the New Testament

12. Conclusion 103

Appendix 1: Musical Instruments 105

Appendix 2: Plants and Trees 110

Appendix 3: Animals and Birds 122

Appendix 4: Precious Stones in Exod 28 128

Abbreviations 133

Bibliography 135

Ancient Document Index 143

Subject Index 148

Word Index (By Language) 158

Index of Zoological and Botanical Names 165

Acknowledgments

THIS BOOK GREW OUT of notes amassed working on Bible translation for over thirty years. To a large extent it reflects my own personal interests, not least the land of Turkey where my wife, Jane, and I lived for nearly fourteen years and which we have visited frequently since. Lectures given at Horsleys Green, UK, and Fjellhaug International College, Oslo, Norway, convinced me that this material should be made more widely known. My special thanks are due to Emeritus Professor Alan Millard, Professor James Hoffmeier, Dr. Selim Adalı, and Peter Stafford for their detailed comments and corrections.

Abbreviations

ABD *The Anchor Bible Dictionary*. 6 vols. Edited by David Noel Freedman. New York: Doubleday, 1992.

AF *Altorientalische Forschungen*.

AHw Soden, W. von. *Akkadisches Handwörterbuch*. Wiesbaden, Germany: Harrassowitz, 1959–81.

AJA *American Journal of Archaeology*.

AJSL *American Journal of Semitic Languages*.

ANEP Pritchard, J. B. *The Ancient Near East in Pictures Relating to the Old Testament*. Princeton: Princeton University Press, 1954.

ANET *Ancient Near Eastern Texts Relating to the Old Testament*. 3rd ed. Edited by James B. Pritchard. Princeton: Princeton University Press, 1969.

ARAB Luckenbill, D. D. *Ancient Records of Assyria and Babylonia*. Chicago: University of Chicago Press, 1926–27.

BAGD Walter Bauer, Frederick W. Danker, W. F. Arndt, and F. W. Gingrich. *A Greek-English Lexicon of the New Testament and Other Early Christian Literature*. 3rd ed. Chicago: University of Chicago Press, 2000.

BAR *British Archaeological Reports*.

BASOR *Bulletin of the American Schools of Oriental Research*.

BBR *Bulletin for Biblical Research.*

BDB Francis Brown, S. R. Driver, and Charles A. Briggs. *A Hebrew and English Lexicon of the Old Testament.* Oxford: Clarendon, 1907.

BEAW *Brill's New Pauly Encyclopaedia of the Ancient World.* Leiden: Brill, 2002–9.

BHS *Biblia Hebraica Stuttgartensia.* Stuttgart: Deutsche Bibelgesellschaft, 1984.

CAD *The Chicago Assyrian Dictionary.* Chicago: University of Chicago Press, 1956–2010.

CAH *The Cambridge Ancient History.*

CHB *The Cambridge History of the Bible.*

CHC *The Cambridge History of China.*

CHD *The Chicago Hittite Dictionary.*

CoS Hallo, W. W. *The Context of Scripture.* Leiden: Brill, 2000.

DANE *Dictionary of the Ancient Near East.* Edited by P. Bienkowski and A. R. Millard. London: British Museum Press, 2000.

DCH *Dictionary of Classical Hebrew.* Sheffield: Sheffield Academic & Phoenix, 1993–2011.

EBC *Expositor's Bible Commentary.* Edited by Frank E. Gaebelein et al. Grand Rapids: Zondervan, 1976–92.

GBT *A Guide to Bible Translation.* Maitland, FL: Xulon, 2019.

HALOT Koehler, L., and W. Baumgartner. *The Hebrew and Aramaic Lexicon of the Old Testament.* Translated by M. E. J. Richardson. Leiden: Brill, 2001.

HOTTP *Preliminary Report of the Hebrew Old Testament Text Project.* Stuttgart: United Bible Societies, 1977.

IEJ *Israel Exploration Journal.*

IG *Inscriptiones Graecae.*

IJNA	*The International Journal of Nautical Archaeology.*
IllBD	*Illustrated Bible Dictionary*. Leicester: InterVarsity, 1980.
JAOS	*The Journal of the American Oriental Society.*
JEA	*Journal of Egyptian Archaeology.*
JHE	*The Journal of Human Evolution.*
JNES	*Journal of Near Eastern Studies.*
JNWSL	*Journal of Northwest Semitic Languages.*
JoC	*Journal of Creation.*
JSOT	*Journal for the Study of the Old Testament.*
LÄ	*Lexikon der Ägyptologie.*
LS	Liddell, H. G., and R. Scott. *A Greek-English Lexicon.* Oxford: Oxford University Press,1940.
LSh	Lewis, C. T., and C. Short. C. *A Latin Dictionary*. Oxford: Oxford University Press, 1900.
LXX	The Septuagint (Greek version of the Old Testament).
MM	Moulton, J. H., and G. Milligan. *Vocabulary of the Greek New Testament*. London: Hodder & Stoughton, 1930.
OCD	*The Oxford Classical Dictionary*. 3rd ed. Oxford: Oxford University Press, 1996.
OED	*The Oxford English Dictionary*. Oxford: Oxford University Press, 1979.
PEQ	*Palestine Exploration Quarterly.*
PRCAS	*Paulys Realencyclopädie der Classischen Alterumwissenschaft Supplementband.*
RLA	*Reallexikon der Assyriologie.*
RSO	*Ras Shamra-Ougarit.*
SAA	The State Archives of Assyria. Helsinki: Helsinki University Press.
TBT	*The Bible Translator.*

TWOT — *Theological Wordbook of the Old Testament*. Chicago: Moody Press, 1980.

UF — *Ugarit Forschungen*. Neukirchen-Vluyn: Neukirchener.

WAS — Erman, A., and H. Grapow, eds. *Wörterbuch der Aegyptischen Sprache*. Leipzig: Akademie, 1955.

ZfA — *Zeitschrift für Assyriologie*.

Abbreviations of English Versions

AV — Authorized Version (King James Bible) 1611

CEV — Contemporary English Version 2000

ESV — English Standard Version 2001

JB — Jerusalem Bible 1974

GNB — Good News Bible 1976

NASB — New American Standard Bible 1960

NEB — New English Bible 1970

NIV — New International Version 1979

NIV2 — New International Version 2011 (originally marketed as Today's New International Version 2004)

NJPS — New Jewish Publication Society Tanakh 1988

NKJV — New King James Version 1982

NLT — New Living Translation 1996

NRSV — New Revised Standard Version 1989

REB — Revised English Bible 1989

RSV — Revised Standard Version 1952

RV — Revised Version 1885

1

Archaeology and Bible Translation

WHY ARE BIBLE TRANSLATIONS so different from each other in places? To the layman there seems to be no rhyme or reason why Job's question in Job 6:6b "Is there any flavor in the white of an egg?" (NIV) should be changed in later editions of the same translation to "Is there any flavor in the sap of the mallow?" (NIV2).[1] Let alone a third possibility: "Does a turnip have any flavor?"[2] Don't Bible translators know whether it was peacocks or baboons that King Solomon brought into Israel (1 Kgs 10:22)? Why has sapphire been replaced by lapis lazuli (Exod 24:10)? What animal provided the leather for the tabernacle mentioned in Exod 25:5?—A badger? A sea cow? Or did the term in question simply mean "leather"? How does archaeology give us fresh insight into well-known verses of the Bible, such as Heb 11:1?[3] Can archaeology tell us what David's harp (1 Sam 16:23) looked like? What is

1. The New International Version was first published in 1979. An inclusive language edition called Today's New International Version appeared in 2005. This did not go down well with the translation's largely conservative readership, so it was discontinued, with a revision incorporating the non-inclusive language changes, coming out in 2011. I call this NIV2, though it is only marketed as NIV.

2. See below 15–16.

3. See below 60, 71 and 66.

the evidence for leprosy in Bible times? Is there evidence for cotton (Esth 1:6) and silk (Ezek 16:10) at the time of the Bible?

Answers to these and many other questions are given in this book.

But how are such questions to be answered? Essentially the answer is "From the ground," that is, from evidence extracted in some way or other from the ground—what can be called "archaeology."

At a first glance the worlds of archaeology and Bible translation seem to have little to connect them. Archaeology may conjure up images of unwrapping Egyptian mummies, sifting through piles of dry potsherds, even an Indiana Jones–style treasure hunter finding the long-lost ark of the covenant. Bible translation may evoke images of living in a steaming tropical jungle with a remote tribe, learning their language, committing it to writing and, after many years of painstaking work producing a portion of the Bible. Or it may evoke the image of an elderly white-haired scholar in a hallowed library surrounded by piles of dusty tomes.

In this book I will attempt to show how the disciplines of archaeology and Bible translation do in fact intersect and I shall argue that such an intersection needs to be more frequently recognized and encouraged.

Defining Some Terms

"Archaeology" is derived from the Classical Greek word αρχαιολογια [archaiologia] which meant: "Antiquarian law, ancient legends, history."[4] In more modern usage it has come to mean: "The study of human antiquities, especially of the prehistoric period and usually by excavation."[5]

4. LS 227a.

5. *OED* 48b. Other definitions include, "The science of the treatment of material evidence of the human past," Sir Frederick Kenyon, *Bible and Archaeology*, 13; "An intellectual inquiry . . . that seeks to penetrate and illumine human experience in the past," Dever, "Archaeology, Syro-Palestinian and Biblical," 354b; and "Archaeology primarily makes use of material remains, which, for the most of human history . . . represent the only evidence," Hauser, "Archaeological Methods and Theories," 216.

The term "Bible" also comes from a Greek word βιβλια [biblia] meaning "books." The Bible is a collection of books, judged by its Jewish and Christian compilers to be books divinely inspired (2 Tim 3:16).[6] It is commonly stated that thirty-nine books comprise the Old Testament or Hebrew Bible and twenty-seven the New Testament.[7] Which books constitute the Bible has been the subject of much debate. Some Christian traditions include a collection of writings called the Apocrypha or the Deutero-canon.[8] These books, however, were not part of the Jewish scriptures and will not be considered here.

The Old Testament was largely written in Hebrew, with small sections written in Aramaic[9]—a related language that the Jews learned during their exile in Babylon. In general terms the Old Testament was written over a period of about a thousand years ending in ca. 400 BC, though, if its prophetic nature is recognized,[10] it also describes events which took place after that date. The New Testament was written in Greek, which in the first century AD was the

6. Although I am happy to describe the Bible as a "collection of books," I am also convinced that the Bible has an overarching message—God's plan to rescue sinful humankind by the death and resurrection of the Savior Jesus.

7. The division of the Old Testament books of Samuel, Kings, and Chronicles each into two books is not an original feature. It was introduced by the translators of the Greek Septuagint (LXX) version since these books were too long to fit onto a single scroll. Eventually these divisions also appeared in the Hebrew Bible. In the Hebrew Bible the book of Psalms is further divided into five books, but there is no indication in the Hebrew text that Isaiah was perceived as being two or even three distinct works.

8. Traditions differ as to which books constitute the Apocrypha. The Greek and Slavonic traditions incorporate 1 Esdras, the Prayer of Manasseh, Psalm 151, and 3 Maccabees, which are absent from the Latin. Of the books of the Apocrypha only Tobit, Ecclesiasticus, and perhaps the Letter of Jeremiah are attested among the Dead Sea Scrolls. None are quoted in the New Testament (Jude 14–15 is from the Book of Enoch, which is not part of the Apocrypha).

9. Ezra 4:8—6:18; 7:12–26; Jer 10:11; Dan 2:4b—7:28.

10. The prophecies in the book of Daniel are often considered to have been written after the events they purport to predict, though this is not the author's view. See my article "Who Wrote Daniel?," 4–11.

main language in the eastern half of the Roman Empire. The whole of the New Testament was written within that first century.[11]

A Brief History of Bible Translation

The Bible is the world's most translated book. The complete Bible has been translated into over 400 of the world's 7,100 languages and the New Testament into a well over a further thousand.[12] Part of the motivation for this remarkable achievement lies in the last words of Jesus to his disciples:

> Therefore go and make disciples of all nations, baptizing them in the name of the Father and of the Son and of the Holy Spirit, and teaching them to obey everything I have commanded you. (Matt 28:19–20a NIV)

and a statement of the Apostle Paul:

> All Scripture is God-breathed[13] and is useful for teaching, rebuking, correcting and training in righteousness, so that the man of God may be thoroughly equipped for every good work. (2 Tim 3:16–17 NIV)

In the light of these verses many Christians are thus committed to translating the whole Bible (or at least portions of it) into all languages.

11. It is possible to argue that all four Gospels, the Acts, and the letters of Paul and Hebrews were written before the destruction of Jerusalem in AD 70. Paul's house arrest in Rome, dated to AD 60–62, suggests that Luke/Acts was written before that date; John's (18:10) naming of both Peter and Malchus suggests a date of composition after Peter's death, which according to church tradition took place in AD 65; while John's use of a present tense in 5:2 "Now there *is* in Jerusalem near the Sheep Gate a pool . . . which *is* surrounded by five covered colonnades," suggests a date before AD 70. Paul's letters would have been written before his death in AD 66–67. Heb 8:13 suggests a date before AD 70 for that letter.

12. Parts of the Bible have been translated into more than 3,300 languages. Scholz, "Scripture," 735b.

13. Greek θεοπνευστος.

The Septuagint

The Hebrew Bible (or Old Testament) was translated into Greek before the beginning of the Christian era. This is the so-called "Septuagint" translation. This name "Septuagint" reflects the traditional explanation of its origins.

The traditional story of the Septuagint Greek translation is told in the so-called *Letter of Aristeas* to his brother Philocrates. Ptolemy II (285–46 BC), the Greek-speaking king of Egypt, wanted every piece of world literature translated into Greek. The letter tells how the king commissioned the royal librarian Demetrius of Phaleron[14] to collect by purchase and by copying all the books in the world. He wrote a letter to Eleazar the high priest at Jerusalem requesting six elders of each tribe, in total seventy-two men, of exemplary life and learned in the law, to translate it into Greek. They were to bring a copy of the law with them from Jerusalem.[15]

On arrival at Alexandria the translators were greeted by the king and given a sumptuous banquet. They were then closeted in a secluded house on the island of Pharos[16] close to the seashore. The translation was well received by the Alexandrian Jewish community and the king himself who, according to the *Letter of Aristeas*, marveled at the mind of the lawgiver. The translators were then sent back to Jerusalem, endowed with gifts for themselves and the high priest Eleazar.[17]

Later generations embellished the story. Philo of Alexandria, writing in the first century AD, says that each of the seventy-two translators was shut in a separate cell and miraculously all the texts

14. The veracity of Demetrius's involvement can be questioned since it is known that on his assumption of the throne in 285 BC Ptolemy II banished Demetrius of Phaleron. Furthermore, one of those credited as being present at the banquet given for the translators—a certain Menodemus of Eritria—is known to have died two years before Ptolemy II succeeded to the throne.

15. *The Letter of Aristeas*, 9–11, 29–34, 176.

16. *The Letter of Aristeas*, 301, does not mention the island by name, where the famous lighthouse, built by Sostratus of Cnidus in the early 3rd century BC, was located. However the reference to a causeway clearly identifies it.

17. *The Letter of Aristeas*, 173–86, 301–20.

were said to agree exactly with one another, thus proving that their version was directly inspired by God.[18] If only Bible translation were that simple! Their resulting translation was called the "Septuagint," often abbreviated to LXX, from the Latin for "Seventy."

The truth surrounding the origins of the Septuagint was probably rather different from the account given in the *Letter of Aristeas*. After several centuries in Egypt many of the Jews were beginning to forget Hebrew. At first, impromptu oral translations of the law into Greek were made, and these were eventually written down. The so-called "Septuagint" was probably a translation made by a number of different people during the third to first centuries BC, but it could well be that Ptolemy II at least commissioned a translation of the Pentateuch.[19]

The significance of the Septuagint translation can hardly be overestimated. Following the conquests of Alexander the Great (336–23 BC) Greek became the official language of Egypt, Syria, and the eastern end of the Mediterranean Sea. The Septuagint became the Bible of the Jews outside Israel, who, like the Alexandrians, no longer spoke Hebrew. It made the scriptures available both to the Jews who no longer spoke their ancestral language and to the entire Greek-speaking world. The Septuagint was later to become the Bible of the Greek-speaking early church, and is frequently quoted in the New Testament.

Other Bible Translations

The Septuagint was not the only translation done into Greek. Parts of versions done by others—Aquila (ca. AD 140), Symmachus (late 2nd century AD), and Theodotion (late 2nd century AD)—have survived. There were also several translations into Latin—the so-called Old Latin version and more famously the Vulgate of Jerome

18. Philo (ca. 15 BC–ca. AD 50), *Life of Moses*, 2.37. Dates cited for authors are those given in *Brill's Dictionary of Greek and Latin Authors and Texts*.

19. A Greek term meaning "five volumed" (LS 1175b), is used for the first five books of the Old Testament—the books traditionally attributed to Moses—Genesis, Exodus, Leviticus, Numbers, and Deuteronomy.

(Sophronius Eusebius Hieronymus ca. AD 347–419). Within the first few centuries, translations of the Bible were also done into two dialects of Coptic (spoken in Egypt), Syriac, Armenian, Georgian, Gothic, Ethiopic, and Old Church Slavonic.

The Bible in English has an illustrious history. The so-called Wycliffe Bible (ca. 1380) was the first attempt to render the whole Bible into English.[20] The work of William Tyndale (executed 1536) had a profound influence on the later Authorized Version of 1611.[21] This version and fifteen later English versions are sometimes quoted in this book.[22]

A Brief History of Biblical Archaeology

Archaeology is a comparatively young academic discipline. In 1799 a gang of French soldiers, who were part of Napoleon's army invading Egypt, unearthed a piece of inscribed black basalt near the town of Rashid, ancient Rosetta, on the western arm of the Nile near the Mediterranean Sea. This text from the reign of the Greek-speaking king of Egypt Ptolemy V (203–181 BC) bore an inscription in three scripts—Hieroglyphic, Demotic, and Greek. After the defeat of Napoleon's army the stone was ceded to the British and found its way to the British Museum. It was this text that enabled the Frenchman Jean-François Champollion to decipher the Egyptian hieroglyphic script in 1824.

It was the French who led the way in digging in other Near Eastern lands, with Paul Émile Botta starting excavations at

20. There is some doubt that the Gospels were the work of John Wycliffe (1324–1384). Most of the Old Testament was translated by Nicholas Hereford. Its source was the Latin Vulgate.

21. I prefer the older term "Authorized Version" for the often used "King James Bible/Version." The English King James I (1603–1635) (James VI of Scotland) is not a role model that I wish to honor in the name of a Bible translation. The story of its production is chronicled in much more detail by McGrath, *In the Beginning*.

22. See alphabetical list xxi. NJPS, of course, is only a translation of the Old Testament.

Khorsabad in northern Iraq in 1843. He discovered the palace of the Assyrian king Sargon (721–05 BC).[23]

The English quickly followed suit. In 1846 Austen Henry Layard[24] while digging in the Assyrian city of Nimrud (Calah) unearthed a black limestone obelisk showing the Israelite king Jehu, or his ambassador, giving tribute to the Assyrian king Shalmaneser III (858–24 BC).[25] Between 1847 and 1857 Henry Creswicke Rawlinson[26] used a trilingual cuneiform inscription (in Old Persian, Elamite, and Babylonian) of the Persian king Darius I (520–486 BC) carved in the rock at Behistun, western Iran,[27] to decipher the cuneiform (or wedge-shaped) writing system.

In 1868 the Moabite Stone was discovered at Dibon in Jordan. It mentioned Israel's king Omri (884–73 BC)[28] and YHWH, the name of the LORD.[29] In 1872 George Smith published the Babylonian Story of Flood (the eleventh tablet of the *Epic of Gilgamesh*).[30] In 1880 an inscription was found in the Siloam Tunnel in Jerusalem which is commonly believed to date from the Assyrian siege of 701 BC.[31] In 1901 the laws of the Babylonian king Hammurabi (1792–1750 BC)[32] were discovered at Susa, biblical Shushan in

23. Sargon is mentioned in Isa 20:1. Up until this discovery he was sometimes thought to be fictitious. Mesopotamian chronology follows that of Brinkman, in Oppenheim, *Ancient Mesopotamia*, 335–48.

24. He was later knighted for his achievements.

25. Grayson, *Assyrian Rulers* 2, 149 §88; Younger, "Black Obelisk," 270.

26. He was also later knighted for his achievements.

27. Kuhrt, *Persian Empire*, 141–57.

28. The chronology of the kings of Israel and Judah is that given in Kitchen and Mitchell, "Chronology (Old Testament)," 273.

29. Albright, "Palestinian Inscriptions," 320–21; Smelik, "Inscriptions of King Mesha," 137–38; Lidzbarski, *Handbuch*, 415. Given the uncertainty of its vocalization, I prefer YHWH to the commonly used Yahweh.

30. Speiser, "Assyrian Myths and Epics," 93–97; Foster, "Gilgamesh," 458–60; Heidel, *Gilgamesh Epic*, 80–93; George, *Epic of Gilgamesh*, 88–99.

31. Albright, "Palestinian Inscriptions," 321; Younger, "Black Obelisk," 145–46; Davies et al., *Ancient Hebrew Inscriptions*, 68; Cowley, *Gesenius's Hebrew Grammar*, frontispiece.

32. This follows the so-called "Middle Chronology" which is the most widely accepted. A key text here is the so-called "Venus Tablet of Ammisaduqa,"

southwest Iran,[33] and in 1908 the Gezer Calendar, the earliest known example of writing in Hebrew, was discovered.[34]

The twentieth century saw many significant archaeological discoveries in Bible lands. Three can be singled out here. In 1922 the tomb of the Egyptian king Tutankhamun (1361–1352 BC)[35] was discovered intact at the Valley of the Kings, in Thebes, Egypt. Between 1922 and 1934 Leonard Woolley, while excavating at Abraham's birthplace of Ur in southern Iraq, unearthed the Royal Cemetery of Ur (ca. 2500 BC). Much more recently in 1982 the cargo of a wrecked ship (late 14th century BC) was discovered at Uluburun off Turkey's southern coast. All three are noteworthy for the wide range of objects and materials found, and are frequently referred to below.

So for two centuries archaeological excavations have been continuing in the lands where the events described in the Bible took place. Massive resources were often invested in archaeological excavation in the lands of the Bible, but one chance discovery arguably eclipsed them all.

The Dead Sea Scrolls

In the spring of 1947 a Bedouin shepherd boy, named Muhammed ed-Dhib, (the Wolf), while looking for lost goats, threw a stone into a cave in a cliff near Khirbet Qumran, some 1½ km inland

---

known only from copies of 7th century BC and later, which records that in the eighth year of the Old Babylonian king Ammisaduqa the planet Venus disappeared along with the moon. Due to peculiarities of the motion of Venus the calendar dates repeat every fifty-six or sixty-four years. Most scholars believe that the eighth year of Ammisaduqa was 1640 BC and thus that Hammurabi reigned from 1792 to 1750 BC.

33. Meek, "Code of Hammurabi," 163–80; Roth, "Laws of Hammurabi," 335–53; Richardson, *Hammurabi's Laws*; Finet, *Le Code du Hammurapi*; Kitchen and Lawrence, *Treaty, Law and Covenant*, 109–86.

34. Albright, "Palestinian Inscriptions," 320; McCarter, "Gezer Calendar," 222; Davies et al., *Ancient Hebrew Inscriptions*, 85.

35. Egyptian chronology follows that of Kitchen, *Synchronisation of Civilisations*, 39–51.

from the western shore of the Dead Sea. The stone broke some clay jars. The boy went inside to investigate and found inside the jars some old leather scrolls which he thought he could use to patch his shoes. However, he noticed that the scrolls had writing on them, so he sold them to a dealer. Soon, archaeologists and the local Bedouin were competing with each other to find more scrolls. The Bedouin, who knew the area better, found more.

Eventually it became clear that a very important archaeological find had been made. A total of twelve caves in the vicinity of Qumran have produced some 25,000 manuscript fragments, some no bigger than a postage stamp. Over the years since discovery these have been painstakingly pieced together to reveal approximately 670 extrabiblical religious texts and a total of 215 manuscripts of every Old Testament book except Esther and Nehemiah. Most of the Old Testament texts were very fragmentary, but there was a complete scroll of Isaiah, 7.3 m in length.

The scrolls date from ca. 250 BC up to the destruction of the area by the invading Roman armies in AD 68 and have survived because of the extreme aridity of the environment. Changes in handwriting style have enabled scholars to place the scrolls in a relative order, accurate to within one generation of scribes.

Searches of sites in the wider vicinity—the ruins of Masada, and the caves at Wadi Murabbaʿat 18 km south of Qumran and at Nahal Hever 17 km further south—have revealed a further twelve Old Testament texts.

What Can We Expect from Biblical Archaeology?

A natural question to ask is: "What can we expect from biblical archaeology?" It is perhaps somewhat naïve to suppose that archaeology proves that the Bible is true. The survival of evidence from the past is random and no archaeological site in the Bible lands has been completely excavated from surface soil to bedrock. Even what has been excavated is often confusing and hard to interpret. Even so, three main types of evidence have come to light.

Three Main Types of Evidence

Locations

Archaeology can identify a large number of the places mentioned in the Bible.[36] Within these places a number of locations mentioned in the Bible text can be pinpointed, e.g., Hezekiah's water tunnel in Jerusalem (2 Kgs 20:20; 2 Chr 32:30), the throne room at Babylon (Dan 5:1, 5), and the theater at Ephesus (Acts 19:29).

Written Evidence

Only written evidence enables us, at least in part, to get into the thoughts of people from Bible times. However, written evidence is not just confined to lands where events described in the Bible took place or to only the Hebrew and Greek languages. Words sometimes came into biblical languages from distant lands through trade, so the text of the Bible was influenced (albeit minimally) by Celtic in western Europe in the case of "carriages"(Greek ῥεδη [rhedē],[37] Rev 18:13), by languages of the Himalayas in the case of "nard" (Hebrew *nerd*, Song 1:12; 4:13; Greek ναρδος [nardos], Mark 14:3; John 12:3),[38] and by African languages in the case of "ebony"(Hebrew *hābᵉnîm*, Ezek 27:15).

36. The locations of all the main biblical cities are known, but the exact locations of such sites as Debir and Ziklag in the Old Testament and Emmaus and Arimathea in the New Testament are unknown.

37. BAGD 904a; from Latin *reda/raeda* LSh 1521c "travelling carriage or wagon with four wheels," originally a Celtic loanword. Julius Caesar (100–44 BC), *Gallic Wars*, 1.56; 6.30; Horace (65–68 BC), *Satires*, 1.5.86; 2.6.42.

38. *HALOT* 723b–24a *Nardostachys jatamansi* "an aromatic drug from a plant which grows in the Himalayas" from the Sanskrit *nálada/narada*; Zohary, *Plants*, 205; Braun, "Greeks in the Near East," 26, or via some Dravidian language, Diakonoff, "Naval Power and Trade," 190.

Material Evidence

Archaeological evidence can sometimes shed considerable light on an object described in the Bible. Take for example the *mᵉkōnāh*, the bronze, wheeled-stand described in 1 Kgs 7:27–37. Several wheeled and wheelless examples from various locations in Cyprus have been found, as well as one without wheels from Megiddo in modern Israel. All these examples are much smaller than the wheeled-stands described in 1 Kgs 7, but are invaluable in helping us understand details of the description given there.[39]

Extrabiblical textual evidence is sometimes cited to argue that some artifacts (such as catapults) are anachronistic to the world of the Bible, yet archaeological evidence sometimes emerges to suggest that that textual evidence needs to be reevaluated. A number of plants and plant products (e.g., watermelons, broad beans, chick peas, coriander, cumin, apples, cotton) and birds (e.g., chickens and geese) can be shown to be part of the Bible's world and hence compatible with the biblical text.

It is often only when we survey the archaeological record as a whole that we see when a particular artifact,[40] species,[41] or precious stone[42] is entirely absent, and thus it is unwise to persist in using it in Bible translation.

Where This Book Is Going

The key question that needs to be asked is: "How has archaeology increased our understanding of the Bible—both Old and New Testaments?" It is that question that will be addressed in the following chapters.

We shall then consider how ancient documents have shed light on the Old Testament text (chapter 2) and how the discovery

39. See my articles, "Mĕkōnôt," 61–72, and "Understanding Solomon's Wheeled Stands," 75–82.

40. As in the case of hinge, tambourine (with jingles), and dulcimer.

41. As in the case of sandalwood, chestnut, and anise.

42. As in the case of emeralds, diamonds, and sapphires.

of ancient artifacts has contributed to our understanding of the biblical text (chapter 3) and has helped us to better define the Bible's musical instruments; plants and trees; animals and birds; and precious stones (chapters 4–7, respectively). We shall then consider the archaeology of disease (chapter 8) and how the Dead Sea Scrolls have shed light on the text of the Hebrew Bible (chapter 9). After assessing the contribution of archaeology to our understanding of ancient geography (chapter 10), the spotlight shifts to the New Testament to see how archaeological discoveries have confirmed details in the New Testament text and helped us to understand it better (chapter 11). Our conclusions are presented in a final chapter.

Why This Book?

Many have already addressed the subject of archaeology and the Bible. They have tended to concentrate on showing how particular archaeological discoveries have illuminated our understanding of the Bible.[43] The focus of this study is somewhat different—how archaeological discoveries of the past two centuries have impacted Bible translation. Some have addressed this in relation to particular issues in the text of the Old[44] and New[45] Testaments. Others have looked at more specific areas such as musical instruments,[46] the Bible's plants and trees,[47] animals, birds, and other creatures,[48] and precious stones.[49] This book is not designed to replace scholar-

43. Books on this subject abound. Mitchell's *The Bible in the British Museum—Interpreting the Evidence* is a good place to begin.

44. The works of Kitchen are apposite here, particularly his *Ancient Orient and the Old Testament.*

45. See introduction in MM.

46. Again books on this subject abound, but my recommendations are Braun, *Music in Ancient Israel/Palestine*, and Mitchell, "Music in the Old Testament," 124–43.

47. I recommend Hepper, *Encyclopaedia of Bible Plants*, and Zohary, *Plants of the Bible.*

48. On this topic I recommend Cansdale, *Animals of Bible Lands.*

49. The paper "Hebrew Gemstones in the Old Testament," by Harell et al.,

ship offered by those much more accomplished in their respective fields than myself. The examples offered below are selective, rather than exhaustive. They at times reflect my own personal interests, but I hope I have selected the most interesting examples. In this book all the archaeological evidence is placed under one roof. I hope that by looking at it scholars, Bible teachers, and translators alike will see what contribution archaeology can make to translating the Bible.

---

is the most up-to-date treatment of this subject.

2

"Is There Any Flavor in the White of an Egg?" Job 6:6

How Ancient Texts Have Shed Light on the Old Testament Text

The White of Egg Job 6:6

In Job 6:6 the question is asked, "*im yešṭaʿam berîr ḥallāmût?*" The traditional translation "Is there any flavor in the white of an egg?" can be traced back to the Targum,[1] the Arabic Version of Saadia Gaon (882–942), Luther (1534), and the English Authorized Version (1611). It also occurs in several modern English versions.[2] It has the advantage of being clearly understandable, but is it correct?

NIV2 "Is there any flavor in the sap of the mallow?" also occurs in NEB/REB, NJPS, NRSV,[3] and ESV. It seems to be based on

1. An Aramaic translation of the Hebrew.

2. Such as NASB, GNB, CEV, NIV, and NLT. These versions are quoted in publication order except that a recognized revision is placed next to its parent translation.

3. The Revised Standard Version was first published in 1952. It was revised

the later Aramaic *ḥallāmût* "mucilaginous juice of the mallow."[4] But this is based on a later Aramaic understanding rather than approximately contemporary archaeological evidence. A similar issue surrounds an identification with haloumi cheese based on Coptic *halom* and Arabic *ḥallūm*.

With the book of Job there is the vexed issue as to when the book of Job may have been written, but there is one suggestion for this expression that would seem to be much earlier in origin than those mentioned above. The site of Tell Atçana (Alalakh), near the Orontes River in southeast Turkey, has yielded an archive of texts dating from the fifteenth century BC. There are three references to an Akkadian[5] word *ḫilimetu*—"a type of vegetable, perhaps a turnip used as cattle fodder"[6]—suggesting that the translation "Does the *ḫilimetu*-turnip have any flavor?" may be correct. The problem that translators face is putting such an expression into any given language. In the end one may have to settle for "the white of an egg" after all—at least it is understandable, even if probably incorrect. This is an issue that is likely to be repeated if any solution, even if technically correct, is too obscure to be readily understood in a translation.

Archaeology can on occasion challenge the tradition enshrined in Bible translation. If, as in the case of the above example, a new understanding is more obscure, or less understandable than the traditional view, it is unlikely to gain acceptance. The examples selected below are, in my view, clear cases of where an archaeological discovery occasions a revision of the traditional text.

---

in 1989 with an inclusive language edition called the New Revised Standard Version. A more conservative non-inclusive language translation called the English Standard Version, based on the RSV text, was produced by a different team of scholars in 2001.

4. Jastrow, *Dictionary of the Targumim*, 471b.

5. Akkadian was a Semitic language spoken in Assyria and Babylonia (ancient Mesopotamia, modern Iraq and eastern Syria).

6. Wiseman, *Alalakh Tablets*, 283b rev. 4; 275 rev. 3, 9. *CAD* Ḫ 186a; *AHw* 345a; Millard, "What Has No Taste?," 210.

The Land of Amaw Num 22:5

The site of Tell Atçana (Alalakh) also sheds light on Num 22:5. Both NIV and NIV2 have "[Balak, king of Moab] sent messengers to summon Balaam son of Beor, who was at Pethor, near the Euphrates in his native land." The Hebrew *is ereṣ bᵉney ʿammô*, literally "the land of the sons of his people." However, NRSV has "[Balak] sent messengers to Balaam son of Beor at Pethor, which is on the Euphrates, in the land of Amaw."[7] This is based on the phrase "the land of Amae" which occurs on an inscribed statue of Idrimi king of Alalakh (15th century BC).[8] Amaw is known as a region of the Sājûr valley in Syria between Aleppo and Carchemish.[9]

Deep Darkness Job 3:5

The Hebrew word *ṣalmāwet* has traditionally been understood as two words *ṣēl-māwet* and translated "shadow of death."[10] *Ṣalmāwet* can be demonstrated to be cognate[11] with the Akkadian *ṣalāmu* "to be dark"[12] and hence "deep darkness" or the like is used in all modern translations of the Old Testament.[13]

Thirty Sayings Prov 22:20

The AV of Prov 22:20 reads: "Have not I written to thee excellent things in counsels and knowledge?" The word "excellent things"

7. This is also followed by RSV, ESV, NEB/REB, JB, GNB.

8. Smith, *Statue of Idri-mi*, line 23, (pp. 14–15) and line 37 (pp. 16–17). Longman, "Autobiography of Idrimi," 479.

9. Albright, "Early History of Phoenician Colonization," 16; Allen, in "Numbers," 891; *BHS* 253n5c.

10. The LXX has σκια θανατου.

11. Representing the same original word or root.

12. *CAD* Ṣ 70a; *AHw* 1076a.

13. So all English versions after the Revised Version (1885). Some (e.g., RSV, ESV, NASB, NIV), however, retain "shadow of death" in the famous Ps 23:4.

šilšôm (in the *Kᵉtîb*)[14] is now often read with different vowels as *šᵉlôšîm* meaning "thirty,"[15] hence modern renderings of the verse as: "Have I not written thirty sayings for you, sayings of counsel and knowledge?"[16] The reason for this change is an Egyptian text known as "*The Instruction of Amenemope*," written between 1100 and 945 BC, which is divided into thirty sections, where 27.7 reads: "Look to these thirty chapters."[17] The section of Proverbs through to 24:22 can also be divided into thirty sections, though English versions do not always agree where the exact boundaries of individual sayings are to be drawn.[18]

Like Glaze Prov 26:23

Other sites have produced discoveries that have led to better understandings of Old Testament verses. Take AV's rendering of Prov 26:23 "Burning lips and a wicked heart are like a potsherd covered with silver dross." The Hebrew *kesep sîgîm* was translated by two words "silver dross," but modern practice is to combine both words to produce *k-spsgm* "like glaze."[19] Hence RSV "Like the glaze covering an earthen vessel are smooth lips with an evil heart."[20]

The reason for this change lies in a discovery made at the port city of Ugarit, in Syria. Here the second tablet of the epic poem of Aqhat, a fourteenth- to thirteenth-century BC text written in the

14. *Kᵉtîb* is an Aramaic term meaning "(the text as) written."

15. *HALOT* 1546a.

16. So NRSV, ESV, NEB/REB, GNB, CEV, NIV, NIV2, NLT.

17. Griffith, "Teaching of Amenophis," 224; Simpson, *Literature*, 265; Wilson, "Proverbs and Precepts," 424; Lichtheim, "Instruction of Amenemope," 121.

18. For example compare the scheme of NIV2 with GNB/CEV. NIV2 has 22:17–21 as its first saying, whereas GNB/CEV begin with 22:22. They divide 24:10 and 24:11–12 into two sayings, whereas NIV2 combines them into one.

19. *BHS* 1311n23a.

20. So also NIV, NRSV, ESV.

alphabetic cuneiform script of Ugarit, contains the phrase *spsg ysk* [*l*] *riš* "glaze will be poured on [my] head."[21]

Heads of New Grain 2 Kgs 4:42

Evidence from Ugarit also helps us to understand the word *b*ᵉ*ṣiqlōnô* in 2 Kgs 4:42. Rather than emending the text to *b*ᵉ*qila 'tô* "in his sack," as do several English versions,[22] it seems better to follow the Ugaritic *bṣql* "corn stalk," hence "heads of new grain" in NIV, NIV2.[23]

To Help the King of Assyria 2 Kgs 23:29

Sometimes more precise knowledge of the historical situation at the time of any given text has occasioned a better understanding of a biblical text. Take for example 2 Kgs 23:29 which describes the events of 609 BC. The AV reads: "In his days Pharaoh-nechoh king of Egypt went up against the king of Assyria to the river Euphrates." This would make Necho king of Egypt a protagonist of the king of Assyria, which is the normal meaning of the Hebrew preposition *'al* "against." However, the Babylonian Chronicle has: "In the month of Tammuz[24] Ashur-uballit (II), king of Assyria, and the large army of Egypt [. . .] crossed the river (Euphrates) and marched against Harran to conquer it. They defeated the garrison which the king of Akkad (Babylon) had stationed inside"[25] shows that Necho was *on the same side* as the king of Assyria. *BHS*[26] suggests emending *'al* to *el* "to." So NIV "While Josiah was king,

21. 2 Aqhat (Louvre text AO 17.324), 6.36b–37a. Gordon, *Ugaritic Textbook* 2, 249; Pardee "The 'Aqhitu Legend," 343–48.

22. RSV, NRSV, ESV, NASB, NJPS.

23. Gordon, *Ugaritic Textbook* 3, §499; Cohen, *Hapax Legomena*, 112–13; Dietrich and Loretz, "Ug. bṣql 'rgz," 115–18.

24. A month corresponding to June-July.

25. Babylonian Chronicle 3 (Fall of Nineveh Chronicle), 66–68. Grayson, *Chronicles*, 96; Oppenheim, "Babylonian and Assyrian Historical Texts," 305; Millard, Babylonian Chronicle, in *CoS* 1:467–68.

26. *BHS* 669n29a.

Pharaoh Necho king of Egypt went up to the Euphrates River *to help* the king of Assyria" is a better description of the historical reality outlined in the Babylonian Chronicle where Egypt and Assyria are both fighting against the king of Babylon, Nabopolassar (625–25 BC), Nebuchadnezzar's father.

The Signal Jer 6:1

Jer 6:1 contains the phrase: "Raise the signal over Beth-Hakkerem." The Hebrew term *maśʾēt* also occurs in an important collection of Hebrew letters, written on potsherds, and found at the site of Lachish in modern Israel. These letters were written just before the destruction of Jerusalem by the Babylonians in 586 BC. In Lachish Letter 4.10 a subordinate commander uses the same word *maśʾēt* when he informs his commander:[27] "Let him know that we are watching for the fire-signals of Lachish."

A List of Babylonian Officials Jer 39:3

In Jer 39:3 there is a list of Babylonian officials who take their seats inside the newly conquered Jerusalem. In older versions such as RSV we read: "When Jerusalem was taken all the princes of the king of Babylon came and sat in the middle gate: Nergal-sharezer, Samgar-nebo, Sarsechim the Rabsaris, Nergal-sharezer the Rabmag, with all the rest of the officers of the king of Babylon." A different combination of names occurs in NIV thus: "Then all the officials of the king of Babylon came and took seats in the Middle Gate: Nergal-Sharezer of Samgar, Nebo-Sarsekim a chief officer, Nergal-Sharezer a high official and all the other officials of the king of Babylon."[28] The reason for this change is an early sixth-century BC inscription of the Babylonian king Nebuchadnezzar, a text known as Prism 7834, which lists a certain mdNergal-šarri-uṣur

27. Davies et al., *Ancient Hebrew Inscriptions*, 2; Albright, "Palestinian Inscriptions," 322; Pardee, "The ʾAqhitu Legend," 80.

28. *BHS* 862n3a.

amēlu dSin-ma-gi-ir, i.e., Nergal-sharri-usur of Sinmagir.[29] This shows that Sinmagir (Hebrew Samgar) is the place of origin of this official. The next official is thus to be called Nebo-Sarsekim,[30] with Nebo, as in all the other Nebo- names in the Old Testament, being the first element of the name.

The Apis Bull Jer 46:15

Jer 46:15 reads: "Why will your warriors be laid low? They cannot stand" in NIV. This, however, is hardly the best translation, as the second verb *lō ʿāmad* is not plural, but singular—"he did not stand." The Septuagint εφυγεν ὁ Απις; ὁ μοσχος ὁ εκλεκτος σου ουκ εμεινεν [ephugen ho Apis? ho moschos ho eklektos sou ouk emeinen][31] "Why has the Apis fled? Why did your[choice] bull not stand?" would seem to be better.[32] It would seem we have a reference here to the Apis bull which was selected according to certain features of its appearance and was worshiped at Memphis in Egypt. After its death the Apis bull was laid to rest in its own necropolis at Saqqara.[33] This different interpretation involves a simple change from the one word of Hebrew (*nisḥap* "be laid low") to two words (*nās ḥp*) "the Apis bull has fled" where *ḥp* is the Egyptian term for "Apis bull."[34] Furthermore, the second term *abîreykā* "your warriors" in NIV (literally "your strong ones")[35] can be read as a singular *abîrekā* "your strong one," meaning "your bull."

We now turn from consideration of specific texts to see how material evidence helps us to better understand the Bible.

29. Prism 7834 (Istanbul Archaeology Museum) of Nebuchadnezzar 4.22. Unger, *Babylon Die Heilige Stadt*, 290; Oppenheim, "Babylonian and Assyrian Historical Texts," 308; Da Riva, "Nebuchadnezzar II's Prism," 196–229.

30. He is the official known as Nebu-šarussu-ukin, mentioned in the British Museum text ME 114789.

31. 26:15 in the LXX text.

32. Hence RSV, NRSV, NEB/REB, GNB, CEV.

33. Griesshammer, "Apis," 841–42.

34. *HALOT* 339a. *BHS* 874n46a.

35. *HALOT* 6a.

3

"He [King Uzziah] Made Machines . . . to Shoot Arrows and Hurl Large Stones" 2 Chr 26:15

The Archaeology of Artifacts

THE FOCUS OF THIS chapter is not on texts, but on material evidence and how this sheds light on the Old Testament text. Among the objects and materials considered are catapults and door sockets.

Catapults

Among the achievements of Uzziah (767–40 BC)[1] king of Judah listed by the chronicler is a reference to the measures taken by Uzziah to equip his army (2 Chr 26:1–14). This section seems to reach its climax in verse 15a which says: "In Jerusalem he made machines designed by skilful men for use on the towers and on the corner defenses to shoot arrows and hurl large stones" (NIV).[2]

1. The chronology of the kings of Israel and Judah is that of Kitchen and Mitchell given in *IllBD*, 269–74. In the case of Uzziah the dates given are for his sole reign, ignoring suggested co-regencies before and after.

2. RSV, NRSV, ESV, NEB/REB, and NJPS are all similar.

These non-portable machines were installed on Jerusalem's walls, suggesting they were primarily for defense. The chronicler then concludes his remarks by stating (15b): "His fame spread far and wide, for he was greatly helped until he became powerful" (NIV).

What were Uzziah's machines (Hebrew *ḥiššᵉbōnôt*)? "Inventions"[3] "war machines,"[4] or more specifically "catapults"[5] are suggested. It should be noted, however, that catapults in the time of Uzziah are generally dismissed as "anachronistic." It has been argued that the mention of such machines reflected contemporary knowledge of the chronicler supposedly writing in the early third century BC.[6]

The Greek writer Diodorus Siculus (1st century BC) in his *Library of History* 2.27.1 notes that πετροβολοι [petroboloi] "engines for throwing stones" had not been invented at the time of the siege of Nineveh, in 612 BC. In the same work 14.42.1 Diodorus remarks that the "catapult" (καταπελτικον) [katapeltikon] was invented in Syracuse in Sicily in 399 BC: "The catapult was invented at this time in Syracuse." This would seem to refer to the specific invention of torsion catapults, where the power is supplied by springs of sinew or hair.

However, there are two archaeological examples from before 399 BC that suggest the use of some kind of catapult before that date thus:

(1) A sling stone weighing 22 kg from the Persian siege in ca. 540 BC of Phocaea (Foça) on the Aegean coast of modern Turkey indicates that the Persians were already using catapults to project heavy missiles into besieged cities.[7]

3. BDB 364a.

4. *HALOT* 361a.

5. Holladay, *Concise Hebrew and English Lexicon*, 119a. "Catapult" is derived from the Greek καταπελτης "a war engine for throwing bolts" LS 767a.

6. Welten, *Geschichte*, 113; Hall, *History of Technology*, 700.

7. Kuhrt, *Persian Empire*, 220n5.

(2) A total of 422 heavy stone balls, weighing between 2.7 and 21.8 kg, dating to 498 BC, have been discovered at Old Paphos in Cyprus.[8]

These stone balls, of course, provide no hint as to *how* they were launched into the air. A simple seesaw-like device may have been used, such as the *shaduf* used in both Mesopotamia and Egypt as an irrigation device.[9] There is no compelling reason to suppose torsion catapults were invented by Uzziah, but neither is there compelling evidence to deny his use of some kind of more basic stone-throwing device.[10]

Bed

Hebrew has two words for "bed": *miṭṭāh* (Gen 47:31)[11] and *ereś* (Deut 3:11). The latter reference is particularly interesting as it is to the bed of Og king of Bashan which, it is recorded, was of iron and nine cubits long and four cubits wide (4 m long and 1.8 m wide). Some have argued that this "bed" is in fact a "sarcophagus" or "coffin"[12] with "iron" being rendered "basalt."[13] However, Og's "iron bed" could be a "bed (decorated with) iron."[14] The best example of a bed contemporary to the Old Testament is Tutankhamun's (1361–1352 BC) gilded wooden bed.[15]

8. Murray, "Ionian Revolt," 484; Kuhrt, *Persian Empire*, 220n5; Williamson, *Chronicles*, 338.

9. For pictures, ancient (Amarna period) and modern, see Butzer, *Hydraulic Civilization*, 43–44, figs. 7–8.

10. The substance of this section appeared in my "Uzziah—Inventor of the Catapult?," 119–23; however, the conclusions offered here are somewhat different.

11. The citation reference is normally to the first occurrence in the Bible. The LXX reads the equivalent of *maṭṭeh* "staff" here, which is followed by Heb 11:21.

12. So NEB/REB "sarcophagus"; GNB, CEV "coffin."

13. So NEB/REB and CEV footnotes.

14. Millard, "King Og's Bed," 481–92. The Hebrew phrase *rekeb barzel* (Josh 17:16) "chariots of iron" may be analogous.

15. It is 1.75 m long, 43 cm off the floor, and has a headboard 69.5 cm high.

Sockets

The Hebrew word *pōtôt* is a hapax legomenon[16] in 1 Kgs 7:50. It is sometimes translated "hinge,"[17] but this is in fact anachronistic. In Old Testament times doors did not swing on hinges,[18] but rather they turned on stone sockets set in the ground, so "(door)-socket" is more accurate.[19] Similarly, the Hebrew word *ṣîr*, also a hapax legomenon, traditionally rendered "hinges" in Prov 26:14,[20] should be rendered "a hole for a door pivot."[21] However, the question of the comprehensibility of a term like "door socket" may swing the choice in favor of the traditional "hinge."

Hook

In 2 Kgs 19:28 || Isa 37:29 the prophet Isaiah delivers a message against Sennacherib (704–681 BC) king of Assyria who has invaded Judah under its king Hezekiah: "I will put my hook (*ḥaḥî*) in your nose." This would seem to represent contemporary Assyrian practice since Sennacherib's successor Esarhaddon (680–669 BC) is known to have put rings through the noses of two client kings, as shown on his stela from Sam'al (modern Zincirli, in southeast Turkey).[22]

A particular category of artifact is the musical instrument; it is to this that we now turn.

16. A Greek expression meaning "once read" is used of a word occurring only once in any given text or body of literature.

17. So AV, NKJV, NASB, GNB, CEV. The NKJV is a modernization, from 1982, of the AV, which modernizes the language in places, but leaves the text essentially the same.

18. Small objects such as the leaves of writing boards were connected by hinges. Mallowan, *Nimrud*, 152–53.

19. So RSV, NRSV, ESV, NIV, NIV2. Pictures: Pritchard, *ANEP*, 234; plates 750 and 751. NJPS combines the two with "hinge sockets."

20. So all English versions.

21. *HALOT* 1024a. It is cognate with the Akkadian *ṣerru*, meaning "door pivot" *CAD* Ṣ 137a. Note also the Hebrew *gālîl* of 1 Kgs 6:34 is translated "socket" in NIV, NIV2, "pivot" in NASB and "swivel-pin" in NEB/REB.

22. Picture: Pritchard, *ANEP*, 154, plate 447.

4

"Praise Him with the Tambourine and Harp" Ps 149:3

The Archaeology of Music

SEVERAL MUSICAL INSTRUMENTS ARE mentioned in the Old Testament. Attempts have been made to identify them with instruments which also appear in the archaeological record—both in remains of musical instruments recovered from the ground and in depictions in art. However, it is prudent to bear in mind these cautionary words: "Assigning them [musical instruments or representations of them] to their ancient names, however, and, conversely, assigning ancient names to particular instruments, is often either uncertain or impossible."[1]

The evidence for musical instruments found in the region encompassed by ancient Israel is impressive—almost four hundred individual pieces from normal excavations as well as two hundred artifacts of unknown provenance.[2] This evidence can be supplemented by finds from Mesopotamia and Egypt.

1. Zaminer, "Musical Instruments," 349.

2. Braun, *Music*, 188.

Lyre

The first musical instrument mentioned in the Bible is the Hebrew *kinnôr* (Gen 4:21), which is generally translated "lyre."[3] A lyre has a box that functions as a resonator and two ascending arms connected at the top by a yoke.[4] Its strings are roughly the same length, but have different diameters and tensions.[5] The *kinnôr* of Gen 4:21 might represent all stringed instruments.[6]

Harp

The Hebrew *nēbel* (1 Sam 10:5) is generally translated "harp"[7]—an instrument where the neck is attached directly to the body and where the strings ascend directly from the resonator box to the string-carrying arm.[8] Josephus (AD 37/38–ca. 100) (*Antiquities* 7.306) asserts that the *kinnôr* was played with a plectrum, while the *nēbel* was plucked with the fingers.[9] On this basis *kinnôr* would fit better with "lyre" and *nēbel* with "harp."[10]

However, there is no evidence for any form of harp in ancient Israel, so it is sometimes argued that *kinnôr* and *nēbel* were in fact two different types of lyres. David's harp (*kinnôr* in 1 Sam 16:23)

3. BDB 490a. The Hebrew *kinnôr* is cognate with the Akkadian *kinnāru* *CAD* K 387b, *AHw* 480b "lyre," which was in turn borrowed by the Hittites as *kinirri(laš)*. It is the κιθαρα of 1 Cor 14:7 and Rev 5:8. It should be noted that for *kinnôr* *HALOT* 487a has "zither"—"a simple flat many-stringed instrument placed horizontally and played partly with fingers of the left hand and partly with plectrum on the right thumb and with fingers of the right hand." *OED* 1357b.

4. Zaminer, "Musical Instruments," 354; Rimmer, *Musical Instruments*, 13; Kilmer, "Leier," 571; Neeley, "Musical Instruments," 616b.

5. Barker, *NIV Study Bible*, 700b.

6. Stradling and Kitchen, *IllBD*, 1038.

7. BDB 614a, *HALOT* 664a.

8. Neeley, "Musical Instruments," 616b; Rimmer, *Musical Instruments*, 19. For pictures of harps see 29 below.

9. LXX sometimes renders *nēbel* ψαλτηριον from the verb ψαλλω "to play a musical instrument."

10. Braun, *Music*, 23.

was thus in all probability a lyre.[11] Of the twenty-eight occurrences of *nēbel* in the Old Testament, twenty-two are associated with *kinnôr*. Both instruments are recorded as being made from the woods *b^erôš* (2 Sam 6:5) and *almug* (1 Kgs 10:12).[12] Three times in the Psalms the *nēbel* is specified as having ten strings (Pss 33:2; 92:3; and 144:9).[13]

It may be advisable to follow convention in distinguishing "harp" and "lyre" rather than adopting terms for two different types of lyre. In passing, it should be noted that NIV, NIV2 do not observe a strict concordance of "harp" and "lyre," where the two are in a list the order "harp and lyre" is normally adopted.[14]

Beyond this it is not really possible to say much that is conclusive. Some argue that the *nēbel* had more numerous and thicker strings than the *kinnôr*, differing in size, sound, number, and material of strings. It is suggested that the *nēbel* had the deeper tone of the two instruments.[15]

Even though linguistically it might not be possible to make a neat distinction between *kinnôr* and *nēbel*, it is clear there is plenty of archaeological evidence, particularly for "lyre."

The remains of nine lyres and three harps[16] from the Royal Cemetery at Ur (ca. 2500 BC) in southern Iraq are supplemented

11. Montagu, *Musical Instruments*, 13, 39; Braun, *Music*, 17, 23.

12. Unfortunately neither of these woods can be identified with complete certainty. See below 51–52.

13. It is perhaps worthy of note that in Sumerian and Akkadian musical notation nine strings are given their own individual names. Kilmer, "Leier," 6:575; 7:473.

14. The references to "lyres and harps" in 1 Chr 15:16, 28; 16:5; 25:6, Hebrew *nēbel* + *kinnôr* are an exception. The same combination in 2 Chr 5:12; 29:25; Neh 12:27; Pss 57:8; 71:22; 108:2; and 150:3 is rendered "harp(s) and lyre(s)."

15. Montagu, *Musical Instruments*, 41, 146; Braun, *Music*, 24. Contrary to this, the phrase *ʿal ʿ^alāmôt* in 1 Chr 15:20 used of the *nēbel* is sometimes taken as a term for "high(er) pitched" BDB 761b, *HALOT* 736a, GNB. Similarly the comment of 1 Chr 15:21 that the *kinnôr* was played *ʿal haš-š^emînît*, is sometimes taken as a term for "a lower octave" or "low(er) pitched" BDB 1033a, *HALOT* 1562a3, GNB.

16. Rimmer, *Musical Instruments*, 14, 19.

by a depiction of an eleven-stringed lyre on the co-called "Standard of Ur."[17] Also depicted are an eight-stringed lyre on a fresco from the tomb of Khnumhotep at Beni-Hasan in Egypt, ca. 1900 BC[18] and a nine-stringed lyre on an incised ivory plaque from Megiddo, Israel, dating to the thirteenth century BC.[19] A lyre is also shown on a seal from Tel Batash, Israel, twelfth century BC.[20] A twelve-stringed lyre is shown on an eighth-century seal from Israel.[21]

Seated lyre players are depicted on jars from Megiddo, 1150–1000 BC[22] and from Kuntillet ʿAjrud in northern Sinai, ca. 800 BC.[23] A stone relief from the palace of Barrakab, the Neo-Hittite King of Sam'al (Zincirli in southeastern Turkey), ca. 730 BC, shows male musicians playing a six-stringed and a twelve-stringed lyre.[24]

As far as harps and harpists are concerned, a woman harpist is shown playing a nine-stringed harp on an incised stone from Megiddo, dated to ca. 3200–3000 BC.[25] Two harpists playing seven and five-stringed harps are shown on a stone relief from Bismaya, Iraq, dating to the early 3rd millennium BC.[26] An Egyptian harpist is shown on a tomb painting from Thebes dating to the reign

17. Picture: *IllBD*, 1610; Lawrence, *Lion Atlas*, 24; Pritchard, *ANEP*, 97; plate 304.

18. Picture: *IllBD*, 1038.

19. Picture: Mitchell, "Music in the Old Testament," 133, fig. 9.

20. Braun, *Music*, 155 + picture. This seal shows an instrument with only two strings, but there would have been very little room to depict more strings on such a small object. There are another nine examples of lyres shown on seals from Iron Age Israel. Braun, *Music*, 146, 164.

21. Picture: Mitchell, "Music in the Old Testament," 128, fig. 1.

22. Braun, *Music*, 147 + picture 148.

23. Braun, *Music*, 151 + picture 153; picture: Mitchell, "Music in the Old Testament," 128, fig. 2.

24. Picture: Lawrence, *Lion Atlas*, 66; Pritchard, *ANEP*, 63; plate 199. The player of the six-stringed lyre is using a plectrum. For further pictures of lyres see Kilmer, "Leier," 577–79.

25. Picture: Stauder, "Harfe," 115; 5, 579.

26. Picture: Pritchard, *ANEP*, 62; plate 197.

of Tuthmosis IV (1401–1391 BC).[27] A twelve-stringed harp has survived in Egypt from the 18th–19th Dynasties (1540–1186 BC).[28]

Flute

The Hebrew *'ûgāb* (Gen 4:21)[29] is a "flute,"[30] that is, a pipe without a reed. In Gen 4:21 *'ûgāb* may represent all wind instruments.[31] The *'ûgāb* probably encompassed both the vertical and the horizontal varieties of flute. The former is shown on a seal from the Old Akkadian period (2334–2193 BC)[32] and an example of the latter was found at Megiddo, dated to the 3rd millennium BC.[33] Eleven other horizontal flutes have been found in the region encompassed by ancient Israel, the most recent coming from En-Gedi and dating to the seventh and sixth centuries BC.[34]

Pipe

Another wind instrument is the Hebrew *ḥālîl* (1 Sam 10:5). It is sometimes translated "pipe,"[35] perhaps more exactly a "double pipe,"[36] an early example of which is from Nippur in Iraq.[37] Eleven examples of double pipes have been found in the region encompassed by ancient Israel.[38] Among them are depictions on an ivory

27. Picture: Pritchard, *ANEP*, 65; plate 208.

28. Picture: Pritchard, *ANEP*, 65; plate 207. For further pictures of harps see Stauder, "Harfe," 115–19.

29. Anachronistically rendered "organ" in AV.

30. BDB 721b, *HALOT* 795a.

31. Stradling and Kitchen, *IllBD*, 1038.

32. British Museum ME 102417.

33. Braun, *Music*, 110 + picture 111.

34. Braun, *Music*, 111.

35. NIV, NIV2, NRSV.

36. Rimmer, *Musical Instruments*, 50; Montagu, *Musical Instruments*, 45; Mitchell, "Music in the Old Testament," 131.

37. Picture: Pritchard, *ANEP*, 62, plate 195.

38. Braun, *Music*, 134.

plaque from Tell el-Farʿah (South), dating from the thirteenth century BC,[39] on a faience figurine from Tell el-Farʿah (North),[40] on a bronze tripod from Megiddo dating from the twelfth to the tenth centuries BC,[41] and on a clay figurine from Akzib in Israel, dating from the eighth to the sixth centuries BC.[42] The double pipe is also shown on a stone relief of the Assyrian king Ashurbanipal (668–30 BC).[43] Other suggestions include a wind instrument with a reed—a type of shawm or oboe[44]—but there is no specific archaeological evidence for this.

Tambourine

The Hebrew *tōp* (Gen 31:27) is often translated "timbrel" or "tambourine."[45] Such a designation, at least in modern parlance, implies that the instrument concerned had metal jingles attached. However, the earliest known depictions of the instrument—on Sumerian seals 2700–2500 BC; on Babylonian figurines ca. 2000 BC;[46] on an ivory box from Nimrud (Calah), northern Iraq (ca. 800 BC);[47] on a terra-cotta figurine from Akzib in Israel, from the eighth to the sixth centuries BC, showing a female playing the instrument;[48] and on the aforementioned stone relief from Sam'al

39. Braun, *Music*, 95 + picture; picture: Mitchell, "Music in the Old Testament," 133, fig. 10.

40. Braun, *Music*, 134 + picture 137.

41. Braun, *Music*, 134 + picture 135.

42. Picture: Montagu, *Musical Instruments*, 19, plate 4 right. Braun, *Music*, 136.

43. Picture: Rimmer, *Musical Instruments*, plate 12. The date of the end of Ashurbanipal's reign is that advanced by Parpola, *Prosopography*, xxi.

44. Montagu, *Musical Instruments*, 45; Braun, *Music*, 14.

45. It was a word widely borrowed, by the Uzbeks and Uighurs even into Chinese as *ta-pu*. Picken, *Folk Instruments*, 146.

46. Picken, *Folk Instruments*, 144.

47. Picture: Blades, *Percussion Instruments*, plate 55 facing page144.

48. Picture: Montagu, *Musical Instruments*, 19 plate 4 left; Mitchell, "Music in the Old Testament," 128; Braun, *Music*, 120. There are nearly sixty other terra-cotta similar examples found in the region encompassed by ancient

(Zincirli) (ca. 730 BC)[49]—lack metal jingles. So the instrument known in Hebrew as *tōp* is more correctly to be termed a "frame drum," i.e., a jingleless tambourine (though practically few languages may be able to make such a distinction).[50]

Bells

The Hebrew *pa ʿᵃmôn* (Exod 28:33) is a "bell,"[51] which was attached to the high priest Aaron's robe and indicated to other worshipers that Aaron was still alive when he entered the tabernacle's Holy Place (Exod 28:35). Bells are shown on the attire of a Syrian emissary, depicted on a fresco from an Egyptian tomb from the time of Tuthmosis III (1479–1425 BC).[52] Some ten bells, 20–40 cm in diameter, from the early first millennium BC have been found in sites in the region encompassed by ancient Israel, including Megiddo, Akzib, and Ziklag.[53] Bells have also been found in Mesopotamia and Egypt.[54] Assyrian stone reliefs from at least the mid-eighth century BC onward regularly show horses with bells around their necks.[55]

Israel. Braun, *Music*, 118. See pictures: 121–24, 128–30.

49. Picture: Lawrence, *Lion Atlas*, 66.

50. There are, however, a number of depictions later than the Old Testament of classical tambourines (i.e., with jingles), e.g., on a red figure Greek vase, 5th–4th centuries BC, (now in the Burgaz Archaeology Museum, Bulgaria); a Roman stone relief showing the triumph of Bacchus, 2nd century AD (now in the Walters Art Gallery, Baltimore); a mosaic showing the triumph of Bacchus, 3rd century AD, from Sousse, Tunisia; and on a silver plate, 4th century AD, from the Mildenhall treasure, from Suffolk, England (now in the British Museum).

51. BDB 822b; *HALOT* 953a "bell."

52. Braun, *Music*, 195.

53. Braun, *Music*, xxix, 196.

54. Blades, *Percussion Instruments*, 164; Braun, *Music*, 25, 100. For picture of an Assyrian example see Rimmer, *Musical Instruments*, plate 19b.

55. Collon, "Musik," 491a; Pictures: Rimmer, *Musical Instruments*, plates, 17, 18.

Trumpets

The Hebrew *ḥ*ᵃ*ṣōṣ*ᵉ*rāh* (Num 10:2) is a "trumpet," specified as being made of "hammered silver," which was used for calling the people together. A trumpet is shown on a stone relief from Tell el-Amarna of the Egyptian king Akhenaten (1352–1336 BC) and on a potsherd from Beth-Shan in Israel, dated to fourteenth century BC.[56] One silver and one bronze trumpet were found in the tomb of Tutankhamun (1336–1327 BC).[57] A trumpet was also found in the Uluburun shipwreck (late 14th century BC) off the southern coast of Turkey. It should be pointed out that ancient trumpets were essentially metal tubes with a mouthpiece, not like the sophisticated instruments with valves found in a modern orchestra.

Sistrum

The Hebrew hapax legomenon *m*ᵉ*na'an'îm* (2 Sam 6:5) would seem to be a percussion instrument. The sistrum[58] is sometimes suggested. The sistrum was made from bronze and consisted of handle supporting an oval hoop, into which rods carrying loose rings were inserted. It is represented on an Old Akkadian (2334–2193 BC) cylinder seal[59] and in actual examples, from Bethel (of disputed date),[60] and from Egypt dated to ca. 850 BC.[61]

It should be noted, however, that over seventy examples of clay rattles have been found in the region encompassed by ancient

56. Picture: Braun, *Music*, 92.

57. The silver trumpet has a length of 57.2 cm. The bronze trumpet is about 7.5 cm shorter. Their tubes are around 1.3 cm in diameter at the mouth end, and 10 cm at the far end.

58. *HALOT* 603a. A Latin term, from Gk. σειστρον from the verb σειω "to shake."

59. Mitchell, "Music in the Old Testament," 131.

60. Jones, "Musical Instruments of the Bible," 112 dates it to the 15th century BC, whereas Braun, *Music*, 88, dates it to ca. 1200 BC. Picture: Braun, *Music*, 89.

61. Blades, *Percussion Instruments*, 161, 162. Picture: Blades, *Percussion Instruments*, plate 59, following page 144.

Israel.[62] Some argue that the *m^e^na'an'îm* is not a sistrum, but a clay rattle.[63] The widespread attestation of clay rattles in the archaeological record begs the question as to why *m^e^na'an'îm* only occurs once in the Old Testament. Maybe it was a popular rather than an officially sanctioned cultic instrument.

The Hebrew *šālîšîm* (1 Sam 18:6), literally "threes" or "triangle," may also have been a kind of sistrum, perhaps with three bars.[64]

Cymbals

Hebrew has two words for "cymbals." *Ṣelṣ^e^lîm* is one of the instruments recorded in 2 Sam 6:5 as being played when David (ca. 1010–970 BC), brought the ark of the covenant to Jerusalem.[65] Another term *m^e^ṣiltayim* (1 Chr 13:8) is only used in the postexilic books of Ezra, Nehemiah, and Chronicles.[66] The oldest representations of cymbals in Assyria are from the Middle Assyrian period (ca. 1350–1000 BC), and also in several examples of cymbals from Ugarit (before 1177 BC),[67] Assyria (9th and 8th centuries BC),[68]

62. Braun, *Music*, 19, 100.

63. Braun, *Music*, 19.

64. *HALOT* 1525b. So NJPS following the Vulgate *sistris*. Blades, *Percussion Instruments*, 163; Montagu, *Musical Instruments*, 51. It should be noted that Braun, *Music*, 42, suggests a "three stringed lute" for this instrument citing the Sumerian ^{GIŠ}*sa.eš-dar* mentioned in a hymn of King Shulgi of Ur (2094–2047 BC). A 15th-century BC terra-cotta relief from Tel Dan in Israel shows a lute player. Picture: Braun, *Music*, 82.

65. *HALOT* 1031b. It is also used twice in Ps 150:5. Cf. Arabic, Turkish, and Armenian *zil*.

66. Jones, "Musical Instruments of the Bible," 107 poses the question whether this suggests that Ps 150 was written before the exile. Braun, *Music*, 108, asks if this change was to avoid pagan associations of *ṣelṣ^e^lîm*. Mitchell, "Music in the Old Testament," 134, however, points out this supposed replacement may not be correct since *mṣltm* was used much earlier in Ugarit (Gordon, *Ugaritic Handbook* 2, §1528) and *ṣelṣ^e^lîm* was used in Mishnaic Hebrew.

67. Mallet and Matoiän, "Commentaire des photos," 152. Picture: 179, fig. 27.

68. Picture: Rimmer, *Musical Instruments*, plate 21.

from Egypt after 850 BC,[69] and from western Iran between the ninth and seventh centuries BC.[70] A Babylonian plaque from ca. 700–600 BC shows a lady cymbalist.[71] At least twenty-eight cymbals (individual or pairs) have been found at fourteen sites in the region encompassed by ancient Israel.[72] The cymbals found are of two different sizes, 8–12 cm in diameter and 3–6 cm in diameter. These different sizes may be reflected in Ps 150:5 *ṣilṣ^e lê šāma'* and *ṣilṣ^e lê terû'āh*, translated "clash of cymbals" and "resounding cymbals" respectively by NIV, NIV2.[73]

In the Babylonian Band

A number of musical instruments in the Babylonian band of Nebuchadnezzar are listed in Daniel chapter 3. This list, repeated four times with some variation,[74] is written in Aramaic, but four of the instruments have Greek names.[75] Thus:

The Aramaic *qayt^e rôs* (Dan 3:5c) is generally rendered "lyre."[76] It is to be equated with Greek κιθαρα [kithara] "a kind of lyre or lute."[77]

69. These cymbals are 17 cm across, approximately 1.5 mm thick and 160 grams in weight. Blades, *Percussion Instruments*, 168 (with measurements converted to metric). Picture: plate 60, following page 144.

70. Picture: Stradling and Kitchen *IllBD*, 1033.

71. Blades, *Percussion Instruments*, 165.

72. Braun, *Music*, 107.

73. Braun, *Music*, 21, 109.

74. The variations, set out clearly by Mitchell "Music in the Old Testament," 135, are minor, such as different spellings of *sabka/śabka* and *p^e sanṭērîn/p^e santērîn*. Such variation is common in the spelling of foreign words.

75. This is not necessarily to be taken as evidence for a Hellenistic date for the book of Daniel. Greek instruments could have found their way to Babylon as early as the 6th century BC.

76. BDB 1111a, *HALOT* 1970b.

77. LS 806b. In the form κιθαρις it is mentioned in Homer, *Iliad* 3.54; *Odyssey* 1.59; 8.248. Ellenbogen, *Foreign Words*, 148. Hence Latin *cithara*, Spanish *guitara*, English *guitar*.

The Aramaic *sabka* (Dan 3:5d) may be a "(four stringed) harp."[78] It may be the Greek σαμβυκη [sambukē] "a triangular instrument with four strings"[79] which is used by the Greek Septuagint and Theodotion[80] versions here.

The Aramaic *pᵉsanṭērîn* (Dan 3:5e) is the Greek ψαλτηριον [psaltērion] "psaltery, harp."[81]

The Aramaic *supōnyā* (Dan 3:5–6), traditionally translated "bagpipe" or the like,[82] is sometimes equated with the Greek συμφωνια [sumphōnia].[83] This is first recorded in the works of Plato (428/7–348/7 BC) meaning "concord" or "harmony."[84] The meaning "entire ensemble" is suggested for *supōnyā* in Dan 3:5,[85] and this is sometimes taken as evidence for the late composition of the book of Daniel. However, such a claim is invalidated if *supōnyā*

78. BDB 1113b, *HALOT* 1984b.

79. LS 1373b. It may be a Syrian harp of four to seven strings, the Akkadian *šebitu/sabītu*, *CAD* S 4a, *AHw* 1207a; Braun, "Greeks in the Near East," 26.

80. The version of Theodotion from Asia Minor, late 2nd century AD, largely replaced the LXX of Daniel; see below 88n38.

81. LS 1752a. The Greek ψαλτηριον is from the verb ψαλλω "to play a musical instrument." Rimmer, *Musical Instruments*, 51, suggests a "vertical harp" something akin to the modern concert harp. *HALOT* 1958a offers "a stringed instrument, triangular in shape, rather like a dulcimer." However, "dulcimer" Arabic *sanṭur*, Persian *santir*, Turkish *santur* is misleading since it was placed on a stand and played with wooden mallets (Redhouse, *Türkçe-İngilizce Sözlüğü*, 984a).

82. BDB 1104a, *HALOT* 1937a, NASB, NJPS, RSV, ESV. It should be noted that the term *suponya* follows two stringed instruments (numbers 4 and 5) which are enumerated after three wind instruments (numbers 1 to 3). If *suponya* were the bagpipe it would fit logically after instrument number 3, not at the end of the list. As Mitchell, "Music in the Old Testament," 135, has noted, apart from one very dubious Hittite example from Alaca Hüyük dating to the 14th century BC there is no evidence for the bagpipe before the beginning of the Christian era.

83. LS 1469b3.

84. Plato, *Cratylus* 405D, *Republic* 531A, and *Laws* 689D (in the latter ξυμφωνια).

85. Braun, *Music*, 34.

is a transliteration of a dialect form of τυμπανον [tumpanon] "kettledrum."[86]

For summary table of musical instruments see appendix 1 (pages 105–07).

We now move from man-made artifacts to another type of material evidence—that provided by plants and trees.

86. LS 1589a. So NRSV. Large drums make an early appearance in Sumerian art, witness the depiction of two large stone drums on stone slabs dating to ca. 2500 BC. Blades, *Percussion Instruments*, 153, pictures: 50, 51 facing page 144. They are also shown on Babylonian figurines of ca. 2000 BC. Picken, *Folk Instruments*, 144. Mitchell, "Music in the Old Testament," 139, argues for "tambour."

5

"He [King Solomon] Described Plant Life, from the Cedar of Lebanon to the Hyssop That Grows Out of Walls" 1 Kgs 4:33a

Translating Plants and Trees

PLANTS AND TREES ARE relatively common in the Bible. Israel's King Solomon is credited with an interest in botany: "He described plant life, from the cedar of Lebanon to the hyssop[1] that grows out of walls" (1 Kgs 4:33a NIV). Plants, trees, and their products are also preserved in the archaeological record. But since vegetables consist almost entirely of soft tissue and are only preserved in extremely dry conditions, outside Egypt there is almost no archaeological evidence of vegetable crops.[2] Their seeds are more frequently preserved. Trees can be represented by their wood and, where appropriate, by their fruit. An important archaeological find in this regard is Tutankhamun's tomb. Plant-derived textiles are occasionally preserved.

1. The hyssop of the Bible is the plant known as *Origanum syriacum*, earlier classified as *Origanum maru*, not the plant commonly called "hyssop" in Europe *Hyssopus officinalis* or *Origanum officinalis*.

2. Zohary et al., *Domestication*, 214.

Evidence for the following can be found in lands where events described in the Bible took place, and can be shown to be earlier or contemporary with the Bible. It should be pointed out that the examples have been selected because there is some kind of archaeological evidence to elucidate their identification, consequently this study is representative, not exhaustive.[3]

It is also worth noting that where plant species such as cassia and cinnamon are totally absent from Egyptian tombs, it suggests that such plants were unknown in Old Testament times.[4]

Vegetables

Muskmelon

The Hebrew *qiššuāh* (Num 11:5) is traditionally rendered "cucumber" *Cucumis sativus*,[5] but the "classic" cucumber originates in the Himalayas and only arrived in the Bible lands in later times.[6] The Hebrew *qiššuāh* is the green-fruited melon *Cucumis melo*,[7] also called the "muskmelon" or "cantaloupe melon." Its seeds have been found in Predynastic Egypt (ca. 3500 BC).[8] It is also shown on several Egyptian tomb paintings, as well as on a piece of linen.[9] The cognate Akkadian term *qiššû* is attested from the Old Babylonian period (1894–1595 BC) onward.[10]

3. Consequently I have selected 32 out of the 128 different plants and trees mentioned in the Bible. Jacob and Jacob, "Flora," 803b.

4. Hepper, *Encyclopaedia*, 138.

5. BDB 903a, *HALOT* 1151a.

6. Zohary et al., *Domestication*, 155; Zohary, *Plants*, 86; Hepper, *Encyclopaedia*, 126; Jacob and Jacob, "Flora," 810a.

7. This, in the small chate variety, which still grows in the Sudan, is sometimes classified as a cucumber. Maniche, *Egyptian Herbal*, 96.

8. Zohary et al., *Domestication*, 155.

9. Wilkinson, *Garden*, 59.

10. *CAD* Q 271a, *AHw* 923a.

Watermelon

The Hebrew ᵃ*baṭṭiaḥ* (Num 11:5) is the "watermelon" *Citrullus lanatus.*[11] This is the Egyptian *bdw-k3*. Watermelon seeds dating from the 12th Dynasty (1973–1795 BC) have been found, as well as baskets of watermelon seeds in Tutankhamun's tomb.[12]

Leeks

The Hebrew *ḥāṣîr* (Num 11:5) is the "leek." It is probably more specifically the "salad leek" *Allium kurrat*, shown on wall carvings in Egyptian tombs, where also two dried specimens have been found.[13] In Mesopotamia, the leek (Akkadian *karašu*) was known as far back as the reign of Sin-muballit (1812–1793 BC), king of Babylon.[14]

Onions

The Hebrew *bāṣāl* (Num 11:5) is the "onion" *Allium cepa*,[15] which is depicted on wall carvings in the pyramids of Unas (2392–2362 BC) and Pepi II (2287–2193 BC). Well-preserved onions from the 18th Dynasty (1540–1295 BC) have been found in Egypt and are complemented by later finds of bulbs placed in mummies.[16]

11. BDB 105b "water-melon"; Zohary et al., *Domestication*, 153, and Maniche, *Egyptian Herbal*, 92, list it as *Citrullus lanatus. HALOT* 4a (in error) lists as *Citrullus vulgaris* (a different species).

12. Maniche, *Egyptian Herbal*, 92; Zohary et al., *Domestication*, 154; Hepper, *Encyclopaedia*, 126; Wilkinson, *Garden*, 59.

13. Zohary et al., *Domestication*, 156; Hepper, *Encyclopaedia*, 127.

14. *CAD* K 212b, *AHw* 448a.

15. BDB 130a, *HALOT* 147b.

16. Zohary et al., *Domestication*, 157.

Garlic

The Hebrew *šûm* (Num 11:5) is "garlic" *Allium sativum.*[17] Occurrences of the Akkadian cognate *šūmūm* show that garlic was present in Mesopotamia at least from the Old Akkadian period (2334–2193 BC) onward.[18] Numerous garlic bulbs, some with leaves still attached, were found in Tutankhamun's tomb.[19]

Broad Beans

The Hebrew *pôl* (2 Sam 17:28) is specifically the "broad bean" *Vicia faba*,[20] which has been found at Jericho in a layer dating to 5000–4000 BC,[21] and in Egyptian 5th Dynasty (2515–2362 BC) burials.[22]

Pulses

Lentils

The Hebrew *ʿᵃdāšāh* (Gen 25:34) is "lentils" *Lens culinaris.*[23] Lentils are first attested at Mureybit and Tell Abu Hureyra in northern Syria 9200–7500 BC.[24] They were also found in Tutankhamun's tomb.[25]

17. BDB 1002b, *HALOT* 1442b.

18. *CAD* Š3, 298a, *AHw* 1275b.

19. Zohary et al., *Domestication*, 156, 176. Picture: 156, fig. 40.

20. BDB 806b, *HALOT* 918b.

21. Koops, *Each according to Its Kind*, 90.

22. Maniche, *Egyptian Herbal*, 154.

23. BDB 727b, *HALOT* 794a.

24. Zohary et al., *Domestication*, 80. These are the generally accepted dates; it is beyond the scope of this work to comment on their validity.

25. Wilkinson, *Garden*, 60.

Chick Peas

The Hebrew *ḥāmîṣ* (Isa 30:24) is the "chick pea" *Cicer arietinum*.[26] The wild chick pea is endemic to the Fertile Crescent.[27] Chick peas have been found in Early/Middle Bronze Age (ca. 2000 BC) Lachish, and Arad in modern Israel, in Jericho[28] and also in Tutankhamun's tomb.[29]

Cereals

Emmer/Spelt

The Hebrew *kussemet* (Exod 9:32) is rendered "spelt,"[30] but "emmer"[31] is the more correct term. Emmer is endemic to the Fertile Crescent,[32] and is the only wheat known in Egyptian tombs,[33] being the principal wheat in the Near East from the beginning of agriculture—traditionally dated to 8th–7th millennia BC.[34] Emmer was found in a model granary in Tutankhamun's tomb.[35]

26. Zohary et al., *Domestication*, 77; Zohary, *Plants*, 83. Cf. Arabic *ḥumus*, Lane, *Lexicon* 644a "to be sour" = hummus. Does this better explain *ḥōmēṣ* "vinegar" in Ruth 2:14? Note that for *ḥāmîṣ* BDB 330a has "seasoned" (Cf. NEB/REB) and *HALOT* 328a and *DCH* 3, 254a have "sorrel."

27. Zohary et al., *Domestication*, 3.

28. Hepper, *Encyclopaedia*, 130.

29. Zohary et al., *Domestication*, 89.

30. BDB 493b, *HALOT* 490a.

31. Akkadian *kunāšu CAD* K 536a; *AHw* 506b "emmer."

32. Zohary et al., *Domestication*, 3.

33. Hepper, *Encyclopaedia*, 85; Kaiser, "Exodus," 363.

34. Zohary et al., *Domestication*, 43.

35. Wilkinson, *Garden*, 61.

Millet

The Hebrew terms *śôrāh* (Isa 28:25),[36] and *dōḥan* (Ezek 4:9) may be "millet,"[37] a rare cereal in Bible times, but which is attested in Babylonia from the Middle Babylonian period (1595–1171 BC) onward, in Tell Deir Alla in Jordan (ca. 1200–500 BC) and in Nimrud (Calah), Iraq in the seventh century BC.[38] A further term *pannag* occurs in Ezek 27:17, which may be related to the Latin *panicum* "millet."[39]

Condiments

Coriander

The Hebrew *gad* (Exod 16:31) is coriander *Coriandrum sativum*.[40] Coriander is mentioned in the Egyptian medical Papyrus Ebers ca. 1550 BC. About half a liter of coriander seeds was found in Tutankhamun's tomb.[41] Coriander was also found in the Uluburun shipwreck. Exod 16:31 specifies the coriander seeds as being *lābān* "white." In fact coriander seeds are brown, and this is sometimes cited as a reason to equate Hebrew *gad* with Arabic *gidda*

36. *HALOT* 1313b a type of class of sorghum grains, i.e., "millet," Arabic *ḏurrat.*

37. BDB 191a "millet," Zohary et al., *Domestication*, 69 "broomcorn millet" *Panicum milaceum.*

38. Akkadian *duḫnu CAD* D 171a, *AHw* 174b.

39. Diakonoff, "Naval Power and Trade," 185 note c. Another interpretation is "confections" NIV, NIV2; NASB "cakes." Cf. the Akkadian *pannigu* "cake"; *CAD* P 83b "type of bread"; *AHw* 818b "a sort of flour or baked goods"; Diakonoff, "Naval Power and Trade," 185 note c. Cohen, *Hapax Legomena*, 118, equates with the Hittite *punniki* "baked food" mentioned with honey in Hittite texts of mid-2nd millennium along with soup, sweet bread, and crocus. Cf. the modern Hebrew "pastry," "honey-cake." Ben Yehuda, *Dictionary*, 245b; but pastries were not practical export products; they would have been stale by the time they arrived anywhere. Hepper, *Encyclopaedia*, 94n6, thinks the term in question is "unripe figs" so also RSV and NLT.

40. BDB 151a, *HALOT* 176b.

41. Zohary et al., *Domestication*, 164.

"wormwood," which is white.[42] This, however, is not necessarily a compelling argument, since the Hebrew word *lābān* may include "brown" or be used for pale colors in general.

Cumin

The Hebrew *kammōn* (Isa 28:25) is cumin *Cuminum cyminum.*[43] It is cognate with the Akkadian *kamūnu* which is attested in texts from the Old Akkadian period (2334–2193 BC) onward.[44] It also occurs in Mycenaean Greek as *kumino.*[45] A basket full of cumin was included in the burial of an architect of the Egyptian king Amenophis III (1392–1354 BC).[46]

Black Cumin

Another Hebrew term *qeṣaḥ* (Isa 28:25) is specifically "black cumin" *Nigella sativa*,[47] seeds of which were found in Tutankhamun's tomb,[48] in the Uluburun shipwreck, and at En-Gedi in Israel.[49]

Dill

The Greek ανηθον [anēthon] (Matt 23:23) is "dill," *Anethum graveolens*,[50] which was widely used in antiquity for culinary and

42. Zohary, *Plants*, 92. Hebrew has a term for "wormwood" *laʿănāh* (Deut 29:17).

43. BDB 485a, *HALOT* 481b; Ellenbogen, *Foreign Words*, 85.

44. *CAD* K 131b, *AHw* 434a.

45. Chadwick, *Documents*, 557b.

46. Zohary et al., *Domestication*, 164.

47. BDB 892b, *HALOT* 1122a; Hepper, *Encyclopaedia*, 133; Zohary, *Plants*, 91; though it is rendered "dill" by RSV, NRSV, ESV, NASB, and GNB and "caraway" by NIV, NIV2.

48. Zohary et al., *Domestication*, 164.

49. Also known as Tel Goren. Jacob and Jacob, "Flora," 811b.

50. LS 125a and all modern English versions.

medicinal purposes. Several twigs of dill were found in the tomb of the Egyptian king Amenophis II (1428–1402 BC).[51] The AV renders it "anise"[52] (*Pimpinella anisa*), which is of southern European origin. It is unlikely that it was grown in ancient Israel, even by New Testament times.[53]

Fruit and Nut Trees

The Vine

The grapevine, Hebrew *gepen* (Gen 40:9) *Vitis vinifera* is mentioned more than any other plant or tree in the Bible. *Vitis vinifera* (from the wild form *Vitis sylvestris*) produces grapes, which naturally ferment to produce wine. The Hebrew term for "wine" *yayin* (Gen 9:21) has clear cognates in several other Semitic languages, e.g., Ugaritic[54] *yn* and Arabic *wayn* (meaning "black grapes").[55] A proto-Semitic form **wayn*[56] is postulated with which one of the Egyptian words for "wine" *wnš.(t)* would seem to be cognate.[57] But the cognates extend far wider to the postulated proto-Indo-European term **woino*, the supposed origin of the Hittite *wiyana*, Mycenaean Greek *wono*,[58] Greek (ϝ)οινος [(w)oinos], and Latin *vinum*. A proto-Indo-European root **w(e)i* "to weave," "to plait," "to twist" describing the grapevine is advanced for this word.[59]

51. Zohary et al., *Domestication*, 164.

52. Gk. ανvησον BAGD 78b, LS 132b. NKJV also has "anise."

53. Hepper, *Encyclopaedia*, 132; Zohary, *Plants*, 88.

54. The language of Ugarit, modern Ras Shamra, a Syrian seaport, destroyed by the Sea Peoples ca. 1177 BC.

55. Van Selms, "Etymology of yayin 'Wine,'" 76–84.

56. An * before a word indicates a postulated form; it is not found in any ancient text.

57. Gamkrelidze and Ivanov, *Indo-Europeans*, 558n21. Pereltsvaig and Lewis, *Controversy*, 193, reference 28, cite *īnu* as the Akkadian word for "wine," but this exists only in a lexical list and a connection with Hebrew *yayin* is explicitly denied. *CAD* I/J 152b.

58. Chadwick, *Documents*, 592b.

59. Gamkrelidze and Ivanov, *Indo-Europeans*, 560n21. The vine is primarily

Contrary to this view Georgian *ğvino* and Laz *ğvini* "wine" from the southern Caucasian (or Kartvalian) language family are advanced as examples of a Caucasian origin for this root.[60]

It is interesting to note a detail from the Old Testament story of Noah. Following his disembarkation from the ark, which had landed on one of the mountains of Ararat (ancient Urartu—broadly modern eastern Turkey),[61] Noah planted a vineyard and became drunk on the produce (Gen 9:20–21).

It could be that the vine originated in the southern Caucasus where grape pips in a carbonized or petrified state have been found at a number of Neolithic sites.[62] Carbonized grape pips dating from the Egyptian 1st Dynasty (3100–2850 BC) have been found in tombs at Abydos. Raisins have been found at the 3rd Dynasty Zoser's (2691–2672 BC) Step Pyramid at Saqqara. Shriveled grapes and pips were found in Tutankhamun's tomb. The vine did not flourish in most parts of the hot Nile Valley. Raisins and wine were largely imported into Egypt; grapes were grown only as a luxury crop, and were restricted mainly to the cooler Delta area.[63]

Pomegranate

The Hebrew *rimmôn* (Exod 28:33) is the "pomegranate" (*Punica granatum*). The tree was introduced into Egypt from Asia in the New Kingdom (1540–1070 BC). It is shown on a wall painting from Theban tomb 217 (dating from the Ramesside period 1295–1070 BC).[64] Whole pomegranates were found in the Uluburun shipwreck.

---

a forest climber and seen to be native in the humid and climatically mild forest south of the Caspian Sea and along the southern fringe of Black Sea. Zohary et al., *Domestication*, 122.

60. Pereltsvaig and Lewis, *Controversy*, 194n28.

61. See 83 below.

62. Lang, *Armenia*, 607.

63. Zohary et al., *Domestication*, 125, 126, 175. For further discussion on ancient vines and apples see my article "Making Some Sense of Babel," 110–11.

64. Maniche, *Egyptian Herbal*, 139.

Apple

The Hebrew *tappûaḥ* "apple" (Prov 25:11) is cognate with the Egyptian *tpḥ* from which it would seem to have been borrowed. Apples (*Malus pumila*), derived from the "crab apple" (*Malus sylvestris*), are thought to have originated in the southern Caucasus.[65] Small apples were found among the offerings deposited in a tomb in the Royal Cemetery of Ur.[66] A papyrus of the Egyptian pharaoh Ramesses II (1279–1213 BC) discloses that the fields of the Delta were full of apples.[67] Several dozen carbonized apples have been found at Kadesh Barnea in Sinai in a ninth-century BC context.[68]

The apricot (*Armeniaca vulgaris*) has been suggested for "apple" in Prov 25:11,[69] but this has received little support. Although one Akkadian dictionary equates the Akkadian *armannu* with "apricot,"[70] this is denied by the other.[71] It is commonly stated that the apricot, which originated in China, appears to have only reached the Roman world following a military campaign in Armenia in AD 63.[72]

65. Gamkrelidze and Ivanov, *Indo-Europeans*, 552n21. It is perhaps worthy of note that "apple" in the south Caucasian language Laz *uşkuri* would seem to be cognate with Sumerian *ḫašḫur* (and Akkadian *ḫašḫūru*). Bucaklişi, Uzunhasanoğlu, and Aleksiva, *Lazca Sözlük*, 934b; *CAD* Ḫ 139b, *AHw* 333b. These languages are separated by considerable geographical and chronological distance, so perhaps a borrowing from a hitherto unknown intermediate origin would seem likely.

66. Zohary et al., *Domestication*, 137.

67. Zohary, *Plants*, 70.

68. Hepper, *Encyclopaedia*, 118.

69. *Fauna and Flora of the Bible*, 93; NEB (but not REB); Toy, *Proverbs*, 462 (among other suggestions).

70. *AHw* 69b.

71. *CAD* A2 291b is dismissive of the above identification.

72. Hünemörder, "Apricot," 910.

Almonds

The Hebrew *lûz* (Gen 30:37) and *šāqēd* (Gen 43:11) are both rendered "almond"[73] *Amygdalus communis*. Almonds have been found at Tutankhamun's tomb,[74] and in the Uluburun shipwreck.

Pistachio

The Hebrew *boṭnāh* Gen 43:11 is often translated "pistachio."[75] It seems that the domesticated pistachio *Pistacia vera* originated in Central Asia and was only introduced into the Near East at the time of Alexander the Great (336–323 BC).[76] However, nine species of the genus *Pistacia* occur in the Mediterranean area.[77] So more correctly Hebrew *boṭnāh* may have been one of these species, being later transferred to *Pistacia vera*. Shells of *Pistacia palaestina* (also called *Pistacia terebinthus*) have been found at Early Bronze Age (ca. 3000 BC) Lachish and other sites in modern Israel, including Timna and Arad.[78] About one ton of *Pistacia terebinthus* resin (turpentine) was found in the Uluburun shipwreck.[79] In practice such hair (or nut!)-splitting distinctions make little difference, as few if any languages are going to distinguish different types of pistachio nuts!

73. BDB 531b, *HALOT* 522b. The AV of Gen 30:37 has "hazel."

74. Zohary et al., *Domestication*, 148. Picture: 149, fig. 39.

75. Cf. the Akkadian *buṭnu* "terebinth" and *buṭuttu* "pistachio" *CAD* B 358b, 359a, *AHw* 144b; Streck, "Terebinthe," 595–96.

76. Stohl, *On Trees*, 13.

77. Hünemörder, "Terebinth," 274. The following are claimed to be evidence of pistachios: (1) an 18th-century tablet from Nippur, Iraq mentions that Ishme Dagan king of Assyria sent pistachio nuts to his brother who was ruling as a king of Mari (in Syria). Kitchen, *IllBD*, 513; (2) examples from Mostagedda and Memphis in Egypt. Wilkinson, *Garden*, 46; and (3) from the Early Bronze–Middle Bronze levels (c. 2000 BC) at Tell Iktanu in Jordan by north end of Dead Sea. Prag, "Excavations at Tell Iktanu," 269. See further Postgate and Hepper, "Terebinthe," 594–95.

78. Hepper, *Encyclopaedia*, 122.

79. Konen, "Shipwrecks," 394.

Other Trees

Cedar

The Hebrew *erez* (Judg 9:15) is identified with the cedar of Lebanon *Cedrus libani*.[80] It was a wood much sought after because of its superior quality, fragrance, durability, and resistance to fungi. It symbolized strength, dignity, and grandeur, and was considered to be the prince of trees.[81] Cedar is attested early in the archaeological record of Egypt. Imported cedar timbers have been found in the ship of Cheops (2593–2570 BC) (discovered under the Great Pyramid at Giza), in the coffin of Queen Meritamon (1450–1425 BC) from Deir el-Bahri, and in Tutankhamun's tomb.[82] In Mesopotamia *erēnu*, the Akkadian word for "cedar," is attested from the Old Akkadian period (2334–2193 BC) onward.[83]

However, it has been noted that "cedar" was not sufficiently long for building purposes or for flagpoles in Egypt, therefore it is suggested that on occasion it may have been *Abies cilicia* (Cilician fir) or other tall growing conifers.[84] It is also possible that, given the wood's aromatic properties required for the ritual described in Lev 14:4 and Num 19:6, some other type of conifer is in view there.[85]

Plane

The Hebrew *'ermôn* (Gen 30:37) is the "plane" tree, *Platanus orientalis*.[86] The "chesnut" [*sic*][87] of AV is not plausible, since it

80. BDB 72b, *HALOT* 86b.

81. Zohary, *Plants*, 104.

82. Zohary et al., *Domestication*, 176.

83. *CAD* E 274a, *AHw* 237b.

84. *HALOT* 86b.

85. See further Hepper, *Encyclopaedia*, 64; Zohary, *Plants*, 105. See also my article "Adam, Linnaeus and Lexicography," 142–47.

86. BDB 790b; *HALOT* 887a.

87. I.e., "chestnut" (so NKJV). Also in modern Hebrew. Ben Yehuda, *Dictionary*, 238b.

originates in northern Turkey and southern Europe,[88] and was not known in Israel in the time of the patriarchs.

Acacia

The Hebrew *šiṭṭîm* (Exod 25:5) is the "acacia," *Acacia nilotica*.[89] It appears to be a loanword from the Egyptian *šnḏ.(t)*, being attested as early as the Pyramid texts, dating from the end of the 5th Dynasty (2362 BC) and onward.[90] The wood was harder and darker than oak and was avoided by wood-eating insects.[91] Its wood was used to make the ark of the covenant and other items of tabernacle furniture.[92] It is sometimes claimed that acacia branches are not long enough for this purpose. However, a 3.29 m long plank that may be acacia has been found at Mersa/Wadi Gawasis, an ancient seaport on the Red Sea coast of Egypt.[93]

Willow/Poplar

The Hebrew *ʿărābāh* (Lev 23:40) is sometimes translated "willow."[94] It should be noted, however, that the now familiar weeping willow *Salix babylonica* came from China and so was not part of the flora of the biblical world.[95] In the Babylonian context of Ps 137:1 *ʿărābāh* would appear to be *Populus euphratica*, the "Euphrates

88. Zohary et al., *Domestication*, 150. Hepper, *IllBD*, 1591.

89. BDB 1008b, *HALOT* 1473b.

90. Ellenbogen, *Foreign Words*, 160; Muchiki, *Egyptian Proper Names*, 256, 343.

91. Kaiser, "Exodus," 453.

92. E.g., Exod 25:10, 23; 27:1.

93. Ward and Zazzaro, "Pharonic Seagoing Ships," 34. The plank in question, T34, could also be cedar, so such evidence should be used with caution.

94. RSV, NRSV, ESV, NASB, NEB/REB, NJPS.

95. Hepper, *Encyclopaedia*, 72.

poplar,"[96] but "willow" elsewhere. It should be noted that the foliage of the two trees is similar.[97]

Almug/Algum

The identity of the Hebrew tree *almug* (1 Kgs 10:11, 12) remains uncertain, as is the identity of the variant *algum* (2 Chr 2:7). The geographical contexts of the examples are significant. The *almugîm* mentioned in 1 Kgs 10:11, 12 are from Ophir.[98] In 2 Chr 2:7 the *algumîm* are from Lebanon (along with cedars and *b*ᵉ*rôšîm* (evergreens/conifers),[99] whereas 2 Chr 9:10 states that Hiram (and Solomon's) servants who had brought gold from Ophir also brought *algum* wood and precious stones.

The tree would also appear to have been used in Ugaritic (attested until ca. 1177 BC) as *almg.*[100] It occurs in a list of tribute from an official named Ybnn. In all likelihood this tribute was sent by the ruler of the Syrian seaport city of Ugarit to either the Hittite king or the king of Carchemish.[101] There is no reason to suppose it was brought to Ugarit from a great distance. Its identity remains uncertain.

Almug is perhaps also cognate with the Akkadian *elemakku(m)/elemaggu(m)*, though its identification also remains uncertain.[102]

96. BDB 788a, *HALOT* 879b; Zohary, *Plants*, 131; and Hepper, *Encyclopaedia*, 72.

97. Zohary, *Plants*, 131.

98. For discussion of the location of Ophir, see below 89–90.

99. See further my article, "Bᵉrôš," 102–7.

100. Gordon, *Ugaritic Textbook* 3, §188.

101. The other tree in the list *tišr* (7) would appear to be the Hebrew *t*ᵉ*aššûr* (possibly "cypress" Holladay, *Concise Hebrew and English Lexicon*, 86a; but *HALOT* 1677a is less committa).

102. *CAD* E 75b, *AHw* 196b from the Old Babylonian (1894–1595 BC) period and onward. Yahdun Lim's (ca. 1800 BC) inscription from Mari 2.17 mentions that he cut down *elemakkam* along with boxwood (*taskarinnam*), cedar (*erinnam*), cypress (*šurminam*), growing on the "great cedar and boxwood mountain" (probably Amanus).

Many translations[103] maintain the Hebrew names, though two identifications are sometimes offered. Some offer red sandalwood (or red saunders) *Pterocarpus santolinus* for *almug* and Grecian juniper *Juniperus excelsa* for *algum*.[104] Others equate *almug* and *algum* and offer Grecian juniper *Juniperus excelsa* for both.[105]

Ebony

The Hebrew *hābᵉnîm*[106] (Ezek 27:15) is "ebony," cognate with the Egyptian *hbny*. The reddish black heartwood of *Dalbergia melanoxylon* (African blackwood), a leguminous tree of the drier parts of tropical Africa, was used extensively in ancient Egypt, being found in Tutankhamun's tomb,[107] and in the Uluburun shipwreck.[108]

Citron

The Greek θυινος [thuinos] (Rev 18:12) is *Callitris quadrivalvis*,[109] also known as *Tetraclinis articulata*. Its Latin equivalent "citrus"[110] has led to the translation "citron wood,"[111] but it should not be con-

103. Such as RSV, NRSV, ESV, NASB, NIV, NIV2, NJPS, NLT.

104. Hepper, *Encylopaedia*, 158.

105. Zohary, *Plants*, 125. But *HALOT* 57b points out that sandalwood is not found in Lebanon and remains uncertain for Ophir (probably in Arabia; see below 89–90). Furthermore, Clark, "Sandalwood and Peacocks," 107, notes that the translation "sandalwood" is based on no old Hebrew tradition. It is a guess from as late as AD 1748 (Olof Celsius) and is supported by an utterly unconvincing comparison with a Sanskrit (an ancient Indian language) word used metaphorically and at a late date to mean "sandalwood."

106. Cited here in the *Qᵉrê* form, an Aramaic term meaning "(the text as) read," which functions as a marginal note.

107. Zohary et al., *Domestication*, 176.

108. Only later was the Egyptian word *hbny* transferred to the jet black timbers of the genus *Diospyros* obtained from tropical Africa and now especially to the *Diospyros ebenum* of Ceylon (Sri Lanka). Hepper, *IllBD*, 1587a.

109. BAGD 461a, MM 575b, LS 684b.

110. LSh 684b.

111. So NASB, NIV, NIV2. Note RSV, NRSV, ESV, NLT have "scented

fused with trees of the citrus family. Originating in North Africa the wood was completely resistant to decay. It was consequently used to make expensive tables.[112]

Fiber and Oil-Producing Plants

Fine Linen

Hebrew *pištāh* (Exod 9:31) is "flax," *Linum usitatissimum*, which was used to make linen. It is a word occurring in the Gezer Calendar, ca. 925 BC.[113] Fragments of a textile thought to be linen have been found at Çatal Hüyük in what is now central Turkey[114] and from the Fayûm A culture in Egypt.[115] Remains of flax seeds have been found at El Omari in Egypt ca. 3200 BC; textiles made from flax were common in Egypt from the Old Kingdom (2700–2136 BC) onward; the weaving of flax is recorded on the 12th Dynasty (1973–1795 BC) Beni-Hasan tomb paintings; the harvesting of flax is shown on an 18th Dynasty (1540–1295 BC) tomb,[116] and flax seeds and linen were found in Tutankhamun's tomb. A most remarkable find was discovered in the "Cave of the Warrior" near Jericho, dating from ca. 4000 BC. It includes a beautifully preserved, colored and fringed linen kilt and sash and a large (7m long, 2m wide) shroud wrapping the body of a dead nobleman.[117]

The Hebrew term *šēš* (Gen 41:42), translated "fine linen,"[118] is potentially ambiguous in English. Most take it as a reference to

---

wood" or the like.

112. Cicero (106–43 BC) bought a citron wood table for half a million sesterces which could still be seen a century later in Pliny the elder's day (AD 23/24–79), *Natural History*, 13.92 (Meiggs, *Trees*, 288).

113. The Gezer calendar (ca. 925 BC), 3. Albright, "Palestinian Inscriptions," 320a; McCarter, "Gezer Calendar," 222.

114. Mellaart, *Çatal Hüyük*, 119–20.

115. Wendorf et al., "Egyptian Prehistory," 1168. These are generally dated to ca. 6000 and ca. 4000 BC, respectively.

116. Picture: Pritchard, *ANEP*, 27; plate 92.

117. Zohary et al., *Domestication*, 105, 106, 175.

118. BDB 1058b, *HALOT* 1663b.

the high quality of Egyptian linen[119] where examples of unusually fine linen have been found with twenty-three threads per square cm. (Modern examples are only thirteen per square cm.)[120] An alternative is "thin linen" which would have minimized sweat from the priests as they labored near the heat of the altar.[121] The term is derived from the Egyptian *šś*, attested from the Middle Kingdom (2116–1795 BC) onward.[122]

šēš was replaced in later biblical Hebrew by *bûṣ* 1 Chr 4:21.[123] This is cognate with the Akkadian *būṣu*, the earliest occurrence of which is from the reign of the Assyrian king Shalmaneser III (858–24 BC).[124]

Cotton

The Hebrew term *karpas* (Esth 1:6), used to describe fabrics in the palace at Susa (Shushan in southwest Iran) of the Persian king Xerxes (485–65 BC), is sometimes rendered "cotton,"[125] probably of the species *Gossypium herbaceum*. It is cognate with the Sanskrit[126] *karpâsa* "cotton."[127]

Fragments of cotton textiles and strings have been found at Mohenjo-Daro in the Indus valley of Pakistan dating to ca. 1800 BC.[128] The Assyrian king Sennacherib (ca. 694 BC) mentions "trees that bear wool,"[129] and the Greek historian Herodotus (ca. 485–ca.

119. Hoffmeier, *Israel in Egypt*, 92.

120. Kaiser, "Exodus," 452 (with measurements converted to metric).

121. Austel, "shēsh," 959a §2473; Diakonoff, "Naval Power and Trade," 172n18.

122. Ellenbogen, *Foreign Words*, 164.

123. "byssus" BDB 101a; "fine white (Egyptian) linen" *HALOT* 115b.

124. Muchiki, *Egyptian Proper Names*, 240.

125. BDB 165a, *HALOT* 500a "cotton" so RSV, NRSV, ESV, GNB, CEV.

126. Sanskrit is the ancient language of India belonging to the Indo-European family.

127. Ellenbogen, *Foreign Words*, 94.

128. Zohary et al., *Domestication*, 122.

129. Thompson, *Assyrian Botany*, 113; Zohary et al., *Domestication*, 109.

424 BC) *Histories* 3.106 notes that "Indian trees produce a wool that is more attractive and a better quality than that of sheep."[130] Cotton may still have been a luxury import in the time of Xerxes and Esther, there being no compelling evidence for domestic cotton production at that time.

Castor Oil Plant

The Hebrew plant *qiyqāyôn* (Jonah 4:6) was traditionally rendered "gourd."[131] It is commonly translated "castor oil plant" *Ricinus communis*,[132] being equated with the Egyptian *kaka*, equivalent of the Greek κικι [kiki] mentioned by Herodotus (*Histories* 2.94), grown abundantly in Egypt for its oil.

An additional comment is appropriate here. When Jerome (Sophronius Eusebius Hieronymus ca. AD 347–419) was translating Jonah for the Latin Vulgate translation he did not follow the Septuagint in identifying Jonah's plant as a gourd; instead he followed Palestinian Jewish understanding and identified it as *hedera* "ivy." There was a near-riot when this passage was read at Oea near Carthage in Tunisia. Augustine (AD 354–430) objected to Jerome's translation not because it was inaccurate, but because it was unfamiliar.[133] It is regrettable that such prejudices still continue today.

The mention of a tree suggests that *Gossypium arboreum* was in view.

130. Hepper, *Encyclopaedia*, 169.

131. So AV, NEB/REB following the LXX κολοκυνθη (LS 826a "round gourd" or "pumpkin") and the Old Latin *curcurbita.*

132. BDB 884b, *HALOT* 1099a. So Barker, *NIV Study Bible*, 1345b, JB, NJPS, following Talmud so modern Hebrew "castor oil." Ben Yehuda, *Dictionary*, 268a. So also footnotes of RSV, NRSV, ESV, NASB.

133. Augustine, *Letter*, 71.

Miscellaneous

The Rock Rose

The Hebrew word *lōṭ* (Gen 37:25) was traditionally translated "myrrh,"[134] which is tropical in origin (southern Arabia). However, all the other products listed in Gen 37:25 are native to Canaan and it is stated that the Ishmaelites (or Midianites) were coming from Gilead in the north.[135] A better alternative would seem to be "a species of cistus"—a rock rose with large pink flowers, prized for its resin. It is perhaps *Cistus laurifolius* or *Cistus creticus*, the λαδανον [ladanon = ladanum], which Herodotus (*Histories* 3.107, 112) records growing in Arabia.[136]

Saffron

The Hebrew word *karkōm* (Song 4:14) is "saffron," *Crocus sativus*. Its purple flowers were used in perfume and medicine. Saffron was mentioned on an Egyptian papyrus dated to ca. 2000 BC,[137] and saffron-gathering was shown on Minoan frescoes from the Greek island of Santorini (Thera), destroyed by volcanic eruption sometime in the seventeenth or sixteenth centuries BC.[138]

134. So BDB 538a and all English versions except NJPS and NRSV. LXX has στακτη "stacte," i.e., "oil of myrrh or cinnamon" LS 1420a.

135. Baerg, *Plants*, 62.

136. *HALOT* 528a. Herodotus, *Histories*, 3.112 states this is an Arabic word. The Greek λαδανον (LS 889b see under *ληδανον*) is the equivalent of the Akkadian *ladin(n)u(m) CAD* L 36a, *AHw* 527a, the Talmudic Hebrew *lotem*, the Arabic *letem* and the Turkish *laden*.

137. Jacob and Jacob, "Flora," 815b.

138. Zohary et al., *Domestication*, 165. Varying dates are advanced for this powerful volcanic eruption, ranging from ca. 1628 BC (Külzer, "Thera," 529) to ca. 1570 BC (Rowton, "Chronology," 244).

Rushes

The Hebrew term *āḥû* (Gen 41:2) "rushes,"[139] can be equated with the Egyptian *3ḥ(w)*. The fact that Hebrew preserves the final—*û* is evidence of early borrowing, possibly in the Old Kingdom (2700–2136 BC) when the final -w of Egyptian was still pronounced.[140]

For summary table see appendix 2 (pages 111–21)

From plants and trees we now turn to animals, birds, and other creatures.

139. BDB 30b, *HALOT* 30b.

140. Lambdin, "Egyptian Loan Words," 146b; Muchiki, *Egyptian Proper Names*, 326.

6

"He [King Solomon] Also Taught about Animals and Birds" 1 Kgs 4:33b

Translating Animals, Birds, and Other Creatures

ANIMALS, BIRDS, AND OTHER creatures occur frequently in the Bible. Israel's King Solomon is recorded as having a knowledge of them: "He also taught about animals and birds" (1 Kgs 4:33b NIV). Well-known creatures such as camels,[1] horses, and lions are well attested in the archaeological record, in other ancient literature, or in art, and so do not need to be considered here. As archaeology continues in the Bible lands there is a growing accumulation of animal bones and other remains, but some animals and birds simply do not occur in the archaeological record. Occasionally cognates with other languages may help with an identification, but as in the specific case of two well-known birds "ostrich" and "pelican" in the list of unclean birds given in Leviticus 11 contextual

1. It is often claimed that there is very little evidence for the domestication of camels before 1200 BC; however, there is a growing accumulation of evidence to counter this assertion. See Lawrence, *Lion Atlas*, 26, and Heide, *Domestication of the Camel*, 331–84.

information given in other passages of the Bible is far more useful than anything derived from archaeology.[2]

Mammals

The Wild Ox

The Hebrew *rᵉēm* (Num 23:22), the Akkadian *rimu*,[3] is probably the now extinct wild ox or aurochs *Bos primigenius*, shown on the Lascaux cave paintings from France and on a fresco from Çatal Hüyük in central Turkey.[4] The Egyptian king Tuthmosis III (1479–1425 BC) claimed to have killed 75 out of a herd of 176 wild oxen and Ramesses III (1184–1153 BC) hunted wild oxen in the Gezira in Sudan. There is, however, no evidence to suggest that the wild ox lived in Sudan, so the Cape buffalo *Syncerus caffer* might be a possible alternative. A number of mummified bubal or red hartebeest and Cape buffalo have been found in Egypt.[5] The Septuagint translated *rᵉēm* as μονοκερως [monokerōs], literally "single horn," i.e., "unicorn,"[6] but in reality the "rhinoceros." The rhinoceros found in Mesopotamia in biblical times was a subvariety of the great Indian

2. The Hebrew term *bat hay-ya*ᵃ*nāh* (Lev 11:16) is often translated "ostrich," BDB 123b6 *Struthio camelus* following LXX (στρυθος), so RV, RSV, NRSV, ESV, NKJV, NASB, JB, GNB, NJPS, NLT. However, other passages where *bat hay-ya*ᵃ*nāh* occur suggest "owl" (so *HALOT* 421a "a kind of owl" as AV, NIV, NIV2, NEB/REB), since ostriches do not haunt the ruins mentioned in Isa 13:21; 43:13; and Jer 50:39 and they rarely make a noise alluded to in Mic 1:8. Furthermore, the Hebrew *qa'at* (Lev 11:18) is sometimes translated "pelican" (so BDB 866a following the LXX [πελεκαν], so AV, RSV, NASB, JB, NJPS), but *qa'at* does not fit and—a fish-eating bird like a pelican does not live in the desert (Ps 102:6) and does not nest on a column (Zeph 2:4).

3. *CAD* R, 359b; *AHw* 986a. It is attested from the Old Akkadian period (2334–2193 BC) onward.

4. These are generally dated to ca. 15000 BC and 6000 BC, respectively.

5. Hope, *All Creatures*, 102.

6. The illogicality of its rendering of Deut 33:17 κερατα μονοκερωτος τα κερατα αυτου "its horns are the horns of a unicorn" should be noted. The AV has the same illogicality.

rhinoceros *Rhinoceros unicornis*, while the variety found in Egypt and Sudan was the black rhinoceros *Diceros bicornis*.[7]

Baboon

The Hebrew plural word *tukkîm* (1 Kgs 10:22 || 2 Chr 9:21) was traditionally translated "peacocks."[8] Modern scholarship, citing the Egyptian *ky* "baboon,"[9] and noting that the preceding word *qōp* "monkey" also has an Egyptian cognate in *gf* "monkey," prefers "baboon,"[10] known in two species *Papio cynocephalus* (the Anubis baboon) and *Papio hamadryas* (the sacred hamadryas baboon).[11] The Egyptian queen Hatshepsut's temple reliefs (1479–1457 BC) from Deir el-Bahri depict her trading expedition to Punt,[12] showing the monkeys and baboons living there.[13]

7. Hope, *All Creatures*, 104.

8. So BDB 1067a, AV, RSV, NRSV, ESV, NASB, NJPS. Parallels were cited with the Tamil *tokai* "tail" and the Dravidian *tokei* "peacock."

9. With *t*- being taken as a preformative. Cf. Arabic *timsah* from Coptic *emsaḥ* "crocodile."

10. *HALOT* 1731a, NIV, NIV2, GNB, NEB. The Akkadian cognate *uqūpu* is used of the monkeys depicted on the Black Obelisk of the Assyrian king Shalmaneser III, 841 BC. *CAD* U/W 204a, *AHw* 1427b. Younger, "Black Obelisk," 270.

11. Hope, *All Creatures*, 17.

12. East Sudan and parts of Eritrea and northern and western Ethiopia. Kitchen, *LÄ* 5:1200.

13. See further my article, "Peacocks or Baboons," 348–49.

Birds

Chickens

The Hebrew *sekwî* of Job 38:36 may be a "rooster,"[14] as may be *zarzîr* of Prov 30:31.[15] The New Testament references to αλεκτωρ [alektōr] (e.g., Matt 26:34) are certainly to roosters. The presence of chickens or roosters is at least possible archaeologically, since they are known to have been domesticated in the Indus river valley in Pakistan by 2000 BC and to have been brought to Egypt by the fifteenth century BC where Tuthmosis III (1479–1425 BC) in his Annals from Karnak records "four birds which lay every day." Chickens are shown on a silver bowl from Tell Basta (ancient Bubastis) in Egypt dating from the late 19th (1295–1186 BC) or early 20th (1186–1070 BC) Dynasties. They are first attested in biblical Israel on the seal of Jaazaniah (ca. 600 BC) from Tell en-Nasbeh which depicts a fighting rooster.[16] Chicken egg shells, also believed to date from ca. 600 BC, were unearthed in the City of David excavations in Jerusalem.[17]

Geese

The Hebrew phrase *barburîm* *ᵃbûsîm* (1 Kgs 4:23) is translated "fattened birds"[18]—a very general designation. More specific is "fat-

14. *HALOT* 1327a, "cock." Modern Hebrew "cockerel" (= "rooster"). Ben Yehuda, *Dictionary*, 295b; Talmud *Yerushalmi Berakot*, 9.2; following the Vulgate *gallo* "rooster" so also GNB, *HOTTP* 3, 143.

15. *HALOT* 281a "cock," RSV, NRSV, ESV, NASB, NEB/REB, JB, GNB, CEV, NIV, NIV2, NLT following the LXX αλεκτωρ. A completely different tack is taken by AV, NKJV, NJPS with "greyhound," which was shown on pottery from Egypt from as early as 4000 BC. Cansdale, *Animals*, 122.

16. Barker, *NIV Study Bible*, 689a.

17. *Artifax* 34/3 (2019) 9.

18. NASB. BDB 141a + BDB 7a and AV, NKJV, RSV, NRSV (also "fatted fowl"!). Note that NIV, NIV2 have "choice fowl."

ted geese" [*sic*].[19] Geese being force-fed with grain are shown on an Egyptian fresco dated to ca. 2500 BC.[20]

Ibis

In Job 38:36 some equate Hebrew *baṭ-ṭuḥôt,* traditionally rendered "in the inward parts,"[21] with the Egyptian *ḏḥwty* "(sacred) ibis" *Threskiornis aethiopica*, the symbol of the god Thoth. Hence NIV2 "Who gives the ibis wisdom [about the flooding of the Nile]?"[22]

The Bird List in Leviticus 11

In Leviticus ch. 11 there is a list of unclean bids, repeated with slight variation in Deuteronomy ch. 14. In some cases cognates with neighboring languages confirm the commonly made identifications such as Hebrew *ʿōrēb* (Lev 11:15) "crow," "raven" (cf. the Akkadian *āribu*),[23] and *rāḥām* (Lev 11:18) "carrion vulture" *Vultur percnopterus*[24] (cf. the Arabic *raḥamu*[*n*]). However, cognates are not always best in determining a definition of a species. In the case of Hebrew *nešer* (Lev 11:13), cognate with the Ugaritic *nšr* and the Arabic *nisr* "eagle," contexts such as Mic 1:16 where baldness and Prov 30:17 where feeding on carrion are mentioned would seem to indicate that the "griffon vulture" *Gyps fulvus* is in view at least in these contexts.[25] In some cases where cognates exist such as *yanšûp* (Lev 11:17) "some kind of owl,"[26] (which equals the Akka-

19. NJPS; see also *DCH* 2, 259b.
20. Cansdale, *Animals*, 179; Hope, *All Creatures*, 135.
21. BDB 376b so AV, NRSV, ESV following the Vulgate *in visceribus.*
22. *HALOT* 374a "ibis," so also GNB, *HOTTP* 3, 143.
23. *CAD* A2, 265a, *AHw* 68a.
24. BDB 934a, RSV, NRSV, ESV, NASB; *HALOT* 1217b, just "vulture."
25. Cansdale, *Animals*, 142.
26. So with variation as RSV, NRSV, ESV, NASB, NEB/REB, JB, NIV, NIV2, NJPS.

dian *enšup/bu*),[27] and *anāpāh* (Lev 11:19) "heron"[28] (which equals the Akkadian *anpatu*),[29] they are of no great help as these species cannot be identified either. However, there seems to be no doubt that Hebrew *dûkîpat* (Lev 11:19) "hoopoe"[30] *Upopa epops* is the Egyptian *qwqwpt/d* and Coptic *koukouphat*.[31]

Reptiles

Creeping Creatures in Leviticus 11

Leviticus chapter 11 also contains further creatures considered unclean.[32] These are specified as moving about on the ground (11:29).[33] Several of the terms found in this list have cognates with Akkadian. Thus *'akbār* "mouse" (11:29), *ḥōmeṭ* (11:30), and *tinšemet* (11:30) are cognate with the Akkadian words *akbaru* "jerboa,"[34] *ḫulmiṭṭu* "snake" or "lizard,"[35] and *tašlamtu* "a type of lizard,"[36] respectively.

27. *CAD* E 172a, *AHw* 220a.

28. All English versions except NEB/REB.

29. *CAD* A2, 143a, *AHw* 54a.

30. So all English versions.

31. Bodenheimer, *Animal and Man*, 55–56.

32. Deut 14 does not have this list.

33. The jerboa listed here is a mammal not a reptile, but included here as it is listed under the general Hebrew category of *šereṣ* "creeping thing."

34. *CAD* A1, 265b, *AHw* 28b.

35. *CAD* Ḫ 230b, *AHw* 354a.

36. *CAD* T 290b, *AHw* 1338b. It should also be noted that Hebrew *ṣāb* (11:29) "lizard" is cognate with the Arabic *ḏubb* or *ḏab* "lizard." Hope, *All Creatures*, 174.

Animal Products

Blue and Purple Dyes

The Hebrew *tᵉkēlet* (Exod 25:4) is sometimes translated "violet"[37] or "bluish (or violet colored) purple."[38] The Hebrew *argāmān* (Exod 25:4) means "red purple."[39] This can be equated with the Akkadian *argamannu*[40] and the Hittite *arg/kamman*. Its Hittite cognate *arg/kamman* originally meant "tribute," since "purple dyed stuffs" were often given as tribute by the inhabitants of the Mediterranean coast.[41]

Both *tᵉkēlet* and *argāmān* are derived from the glands of shellfish. *Tᵉkēlet* comes from the *Murex brandaris*, which lives at a depth of 10–15 m, and *argāmān* from the *Murex trunculus*, which prefers shallower water.[42] Large heaps of discarded shells of these species have been found at Shiqmona near Haifa in Israel, Sarepta in Lebanon, and Ugarit in Syria.[43]

The extraction of glands taken from shellfish was painstaking. Dye had to be used immediately,[44] it could not be stored. Ten thousand shells would be needed to produce a single gram of crude dye.[45] Consequently purple-dyed textiles were affordable only to the wealthy elite. At Rome, purple was also a symbol denoting political

37. BDB 1067a.

38. *HALOT* 1733a.

39. BDB 7a, *HALOT* 84b "wool dyed with red purple."

40. *CAD* A2, 253a, *AHw* 67a. Ugaritic *argmn*.

41. Ellenbogen, *Foreign Words*, 38–39. The word was later the origin of Arabic *urjuwān*, Persian *arğavān* and Turkish *erguvan*. The latter is also used of the Judas tree *Cercis siliquastrum* known for its brilliant purple blossom.

42. Culcian, "Phoenicia," 476. However Firmage, "Zoology," 1149a argues for reverse identifications, pointing out that the determination of the color of the dye depends on a number of variables including the sex of the snails.

43. Firmage, Zoology," 1148b.

44. Aristotle, *History of Animals*, 547a.26–28.

45. Schneider, "Purple," 232 (figure is simplified); Firmage, "Zoology," 1149a, also points out that very little dye is actually needed to color cloth.

rank.[46] In the Roman Empire the purple robe became part of the regalia of the emperor. By the fifth century AD private individuals were strictly forbidden to own garments dyed purple.[47]

Just before his crucifixion Jesus was dressed in a purple robe (Greek πορφυραν [porphuran] Mark 15:17 and πορφυρουν [porphuroun][48] John 19:2) but it should be noted that Matthew 27:28 sees the color of the robe differently as "scarlet" (Greek κοκκινος [kokkinos]),[49] which was used as a cheap substitute for purple.[50] It may be that the robe was a "tacky imitation," rather than the genuine article that Mark and John perceived.

Silk

A case where archaeological and textual evidence may provide different conclusions is that of the Hebrew word *mešî*, sometimes translated "silk" in Ezek 16:10, 13 (early 6th century BC).[51] Other translations,[52] perhaps aware that the earliest western allusion to silk is in the writings of Aristotle (384–22 BC),[53] avoid this rendering here. However, there would seem to be archaeological evidence for silk prior to Aristotle. Carbonized remains of silk textiles dating from ca. 750 BC have been found at Toprakkale near Van in eastern

46. Pliny, *Natural History*, 9.127.

47. *Codex Theodosianus*, 10.20.18 and 10.21.3.

48. This word has a venerable history. In the form *popureja* it occurs in Mycenaean Greek, on one example (x 976) being linked with the word *wanakatero* "kingly." It is also used by Homer, e.g., *Iliad* 8.221 and *Odyssey* 19.225. Chadwick, *Documents*, 321, 573a.

49. It was used on a 2nd-century AD papyrus listing the accounts of a pawnshop. Kenyon, *Greek Papyri*, 2:246. Papyrus 193 verso 22.

50. Mann, *Matthew*, 346.

51. AV, NKJV, RSV, ESV, NASB, NJPS. Alternative meanings might be provided by the Egyptian *mśy* "a kind of garment" from the New Kingdom onward (1540 BC onward): Rabin, "Hittite Words in Hebrew," 129; Muchiki, *Egyptian Proper Names*, 250, 335 or the Hittite *maššiya* "shawl" *CHD* 3, 203b.

52. REB, NIV, NIV2, NRSV.

53. Aristotle, *History of Animals*, 551b.16.

Turkey,[54] and threads from the Chinese silkworm *Bombyx mori* have been found at Athens in a grave dated to the late fifth century BC.[55] These discoveries should perhaps caution us from ruling out "silk" completely in Ezekiel. The silk found near Van may have been imported from China, but there was also a "home-grown" silk produced by the moth *Pachypasa otus*. This fed on cypress and oak trees and formed the basis of silk industries on the Greek island of Cos and at Sidon in Lebanon. The silk produced by these worms was transparent, a property not shared by Chinese silk.[56] The silk (σιρικος [sirikos]) mentioned in Rev 18:12 could be of either type. The Chinese silkworm *Bombyx mori*, which fed on mulberry trees, was not introduced to the Byzantine Empire until AD 552.[57]

Sea Cow or Leather

The Hebrew term *taḥaš* (Exod 25:5) has been equated with the Arabic *tuḥas* "dugong" or "sea cow."[58] An alternative is derived from the Egyptian *ṯhś* "leather"—so "durable leather,"[59] or "fine leather"[60] are suggested.

Onycha

The Hebrew word *šeḥēlet* (Exod 30:34) is obscure. It occurs in a list of spices, blended together to make incense. It is generally

54. Barnett, "Urartu," 367; Lang, *Armenia*, 96.

55. Grave 73 of the Kerameikos Necropolis in Athens. Pekridou-Gorecki, "Silk," 463.

56. Hepper, *Encylopaedia*, 169.

57. Procopius (ca. AD 507–55), *History of the Wars*, 8.17.1–7.

58. Certainly more plausible than the AV and NKJV's "badger." Cansdale, *Animals*, 139, notes that the dugong *Helicore helicore*, variously called *Dugong dugong*, was fairly plentiful in the Gulf of Aqaba until the beginning of the 19th century. The "porpoise" (NASB) and "dolphin" (NJPS) are only found in the open sea.

59. NIV2.

60. NRSV.

translated "onycha" following the Septuagint.[61] This is defined as "*Blatta byzantina*, the horny operculum or shield attached to the foot of many shellfish by which they close the aperture of their shell when they have withdrawn into it."[62]

But its presence in a list of vegetable products may be sufficient to cast doubt on this identification, as Hepper has noted: "It is more likely to have been a fragrant plant, the identity of which is still not positively known."[63] It may be cognate with the Akkadian *šeḫlātu*, attested in Mari in Syria in the early second millennium BC, a "foodstuff"[64] or "vegetable,"[65] and with Ugaritic *šḥlt* "a certain vegetable."[66] A more specific alternative may be an equation with the Hittite *zaḫḫeli* and the Akkadian *sahlû, sahlûtu* meaning "cress."[67]

Ivory

Even though elephants do not appear in the Bible, the elephant's most valuable product ivory certainly does. Ivory is simply called *šēn* "tooth" in the Old Testament. This ivory was used to make a variety of objects as the following table illustrates:

Reference	Date BC	Object Made from Ivory
1 Kgs 10:18 ǁ 2 Chr 9:17	ca. 950	Solomon's throne
Song 5:14	ca. 950	Solomon's description of lover's body

61. BDB 1006a, *HALOT* 1462a.
62. Tristam, *Natural History*, 297; Cansdale, *Animals*, 232.
63. Hepper, *Encyclopaedia*, 142.
64. *CAD* Š2 264a.
65. *AHw* 1209a.
66. Gordon, *Ugaritic Textbook* 3, §2397.
67. Ertem, *Anadolu'sunun Florası*, 54; *CAD* S 62a; *AHw* 1009b.

Reference	Date BC	Object Made from Ivory
Song 7:4	ca. 950	Solomon's description of beloved's neck
Ps 45:8	??	palace adornment
1 Kgs 22:39	ca. 850	Ahab's palace adornment
Amos 3:15	ca. 750	Jeroboam II's palace adornment
Amos 6:4	ca. 750	inlay for a bed
Ezek 27:6	586	inlay for a ship's deck
Ezek 27:15	586	ivory tusks being traded

However, there are two further examples of ivory where the elephant might just have made its mark in the biblical text. In 1 Kgs 10:22 and || 2 Chr 9:21 we find the word *šenhabbîm*. *šēn* "ivory" is compounded with the plural noun *habbîm*, which can be compared with Egyptian *'bw* "elephant."[68] Impressive assemblages of elephant ivories, dating from the ninth to the eighth centuries BC, have been found in Nimrud (Calah) in Assyria and Samaria, capital of the northern kingdom of Israel. The sources of this material are uncertain because it is difficult to differentiate between ivory of African, Indian, or local Syrian elephants after centuries of burial.[69]

The Assyrian king Tiglath-pileser I (1114–1076 BC) boasts of killing ten strong bull elephants in the land of Harran and of capturing four live elephants in the region of the Habur River.[70]

68. This may reappear in *ebur* the Latin word for "ivory."

69. Bienkowski, in *DANE* 158a.

70. The Annals of Tiglath-pileser I, 6.70, 72. Grayson, *Assyrian Rulers* 1, 26.

The now extinct Syrian elephant *Elephas maximus asurus*, which was a subspecies of the Indian elephant *Elephas maximus indicus*, is shown in a painting from the fifteenth-century BC tomb of the Egyptian vizier Rekhmire in Thebes. On the Black Obelisk of the Assyrian king Shalmaneser III, found at the Assyrian city of Nimrud and dating from 841 BC, an elephant is depicted. The accompanying inscription says that Shalmaneser received his female elephants as tribute from Egypt,[71] suggesting that the elephant in question was the now extinct North African elephant *Loxodonta africana pharaoensis*.[72]

For the summary table see appendix 3 (pages 123–27)

Another type of material evidence is that which concerns precious and semiprecious stones. It is to this that we now turn.

71. Grayson, *Assyrian Rulers* 2, 150 §89; Younger, "Black Obelisk," 270.

72. This section is an abridged version of my article, "Elephants in the Bible," 13–15.

7

"They Will Sparkle in His Land like Jewels in a Crown" Zech 9:16b

Translating Precious Stones

STONES, PRECIOUS OR OTHERWISE, preserve well in the archaeological record. The names of a number of precious and semiprecious stones occur in the Bible. In the Old Testament there is a list of twelve stones mounted on the high priest's breastplate (Exod 28:17–20); nine of these are repeated in a description of the king of Tyre (Ezek 28:13).[1] In the New Testament the foundations of the New Jerusalem are recorded as being made of twelve types of precious stone (Rev 21:19–20).[2]

The precise identity of some of the precious stones in the high priest's breastplate remains uncertain, yet archaeological evidence can help identify at least some of them.

1. Harell et al., "Hebrew Gemstones," argue that in Exod 28 the stones were selected for their engravability rather than their preciousness.

2. Eight out of the twelve stones listed in Revelation occur in the LXX rendering of Exod 28:17–20.

Some Identifications Not Substantiated by Archaeology

Firstly, we should note that some of the traditional identifications cannot be substantiated by archaeology.

Bāreqet (Exod 28:17c) is sometimes translated "emerald."[3] However, "emerald" is not found in the Old Testament period.[4]

Sappîr (Exod 24:10; 28:18b) is traditionally translated "sapphire."[5] However, modern "sapphire" (blue corundum)[6] was scarcely known to the ancients.[7] It was certainly unknown in Egypt around 1400 BC when the Israelites may have left Egypt.[8] The term lapis lazuli is to be preferred.[9] This was used widely in the ancient world, and was obtained from Badakshan in northeast Afghanistan, being attested as early as 2500 BC on the celebrated "Standard of Ur."[10] Lapis lazuli cylinder seals of Mesopotamian origin have been found in the Tod treasure of Amenemhat II (1917–1882 BC) from near Thebes in Egypt and among a cache of objects found at Thebes in Greece. One seal was inscribed with the name of the Kassite king of Babylon Burnaburiash II (1359–1333 BC).[11]

Similarly, *yāhᵃlōm* (18c) is sometimes translated "diamond,"[12] but the modern diamond was probably unknown in Old Testament

3. BDB 140b, *HALOT* 162b; (*HALOT* also lists "dark green beryl") so NASB, NJPS, NRSV.

4. Harell et al., "Hebrew Gemstones," 16. For identifications of *bāreqet*, see below 73 and 129.

5. BDB 705b. Greek σαπφειρος. LS 1374b. Cf. also σαπφιρυον, which may have been an intermediate stage between the Indian and Semitic. Ellenbogen, *Foreign Words*, 125.

6. Crystallized alumina of various colors, with great hardness, used as an abrasive and as gems. *OED* 230a.

7. Marshall, *IllBD*, 785.

8. Kaiser, "Exodus," 450. This presupposes the so-called "early exodus" ca. 1446 BC (based on 1 Kgs 6:1).

9. *HALOT* 764b, so NIV2, NLT.

10. Picture: *IllBD*, 1610; Lawrence, *Lion Atlas*, 24.

11. Collon, *Seals*, 33–35.

12. RSV, ESV, NASB, CEV which is equivalent to the "moonstone" of NRSV and NLT. Note also Hebrew *šāmîr* Jer 17:1; Ezek 3:9; and Zech 7:12

times, the first reference to it apparently being in Manilius's (1st century AD) *Astronomicon* 4.926.[13]

Cognates with Sanskrit, the ancient language of India, have been advanced to identify three of the stones: *piṭdāh* (17b) was equated with *pita* "yellow,"[14] *bāreqet* (17c) with *markata* "emerald,"[15] and *sappîr* (18b) with *sanipriya* "sapphire."[16] However, as we have already noted, there is no archaeological evidence in the Old Testament period for either "emerald" or "sapphire."[17]

Cognates with Egyptian

A number of cognates are now advanced with Egyptian, which would seem more plausible, given Egypt's geographical and historical proximity to the world of the Old Testament.

Piṭdāh (17b) may be cognate with the Egyptian *p3ddt* "haematite," a form of red iron ore, which derives its name from the appearance of dried blood.[18]

Nōpek (18a) would seem to be cognate with the Egyptian *mfk(3.t)* "green/blue turquoise."[19] It is to be noted that the production of turquoise stops at end of the Egyptian New Kingdom (1070 BC), suggesting a lower limit to the composition of the list.[20]

---

is also translated "diamond" by RSV, ESV, NASB, and CEV (in Ezek 3:9), the same observation applies to this word too. Harell et al., "Hebrew Gemstones," 38 suggest "emery" for *šāmîr*.

13. Marshall, *IllBD*, 783b. The Greek αδαμας means "the invincible." Hünemörder, "Precious Stones," 795.

14. As cited in BDB 809a; (also *HALOT* 924b); Harell et al., "Hebrew Gemstones," 12.

15. As cited in BDB 140b.

16. As cited in *HALOT* 764b.

17. See above 71.

18. Hünemörder, "Haematite," 1090.

19. Muchiki, *Egyptian Proper Names*, 337. Harell et al., "Hebrew Gemstones," 17. Hence "turquoise" in NASB, NIV, NIV2, NJPS, NRSV.

20. Harell et al., "Hebrew Gemstones," 17.

Lešem (19a) would seem to be cognate with the Egyptian *nšm.t* "feldspar"—either white-blue or green.[21] It is mentioned by Tuthmosis III (1479–1425 BC). Furthermore, green feldspar beads were found in Tutankhamun's tomb.[22]

Aḥlāmāh (19c), traditionally translated "amethyst,"[23] may be equated with the Egyptian *ḫnm.t* "red jasper"[24]—a red, precious stone attested from the 18th Dynasty (1540 BC) onward. This stone was brought to Egypt from Nubia, the region south from the first cataract at Aswan[25] to the junction of Nile at Khartoum, hence its name is probably derived from some African language.[26]

Cognates with Akkadian

Similarly, cognates for other precious stones can be advanced from Akkadian.

Bāreqet (17c), perhaps "beryl,"[27] may be cognate with the Akkadian *burallu*, the identity of which is not known.[28]

Yāhᵃlōm (18c) may be cognate with the Akkadian *ḫulālu*, the identity of which is also not known.[29]

21. Ellenbogen, *Foreign Words*, 97; Lambdin, "Egyptian Loan Words," 152a; Harris, *Lexicographical Studies*, 115, 231; Muchiki, *Egyptian Proper Names*, 338. Note Harell et al., "Hebrew Gemstones," 23, suggest "amazonite," i.e., "green feldspar."

22. Harell et al., "Hebrew Gemstones," 22, 23.

23. BDB 29a "amethyst," *HALOT* 34b, so RSV, NRSV, ESV, NASB, NIV, NIV2. Gk. αμεθυστος. BAGD 52a, LS 74b "that which does not make one drunk," was supposed to prevent intoxication. Hünemörder, "Precious Stones," 795.

24. Muchiki, *Egyptian Proper Names*, 238.

25. For Aswan see below 90.

26. Ellenbogen, *Foreign Words*, 22. Harell et al., "Hebrew Gemstones," 25, suggest "a reddish stone, probably jasper."

27. So NIV, NIV2. "Emerald" of NASB, NJPS, NRSV is ruled out; see above 71.

28. *HALOT* 162b; *CAD* B 326b (which just offers "stone bowl"); *AHw* 139b.

29. Harell et al., "Hebrew Gemstones," 43. *CAD* Ḫ 226b; *AHw* 353b.

Šᵉbô (19b), traditionally rendered "agate,"[30] is cognate with the Akkadian *šubû*, perhaps "agate."[31] Agate has been found in the Royal Cemetery of Ur and the Uluburun shipwreck. Agate seems to have been obtained from the west coast of India.[32]

Šōham (20b), traditionally translated "onyx,"[33] may be cognate with the Akkadian *sāmtu*/sā*mu*.[34]

Yašpēh (20c), translated "jasper,"[35] is to be equated with the Akkadian *(j)ašpû*, attested in a letter of Tushratta king of Mitanni[36] to the Egyptian king Amenophis III (1391–1353 BC).[37] This suggests a Hurrian (eastern Turkey) origin for the word.[38]

Other Terms

The first stone in the list *ōdem* (17a) has no clear cognates, but the root *ʾdm* is common Semitic meaning "to be red." It is probably carnelian, a red stone, probably of Indian origin, and known from the Royal Cemetery of Ur[39] and the Uluburun shipwreck.

The data presented above is summarized in the table cited as an appendix 4 which also lists a recent identification of all the

30. BDB 986a, *HALOT* 1383a and all English versions.

31. *CAD* Š3 185b; *AHw* 1258a, a stone, perhaps "agate." Sumerian *šuba* in lexical lists is *arqu* (yellow/green) and *sāmu* (red/brown). Cohen, *Hapax Legomena*, 128.

32. Collon, *Seals*, 35.

33. A kind of chalcedony with different colors in layers. *OED* 766b.

34. So Harell et al., "Hebrew Gemstones," 44; *CAD* S 121b "carnelian" a red stone. See below 129.

35. BDB 448b, *HALOT* 449a and all English versions.

36. Located in eastern Turkey, northern Syria.

37. Amarna Letter 22.4.6. Moran, *Amarna Letters*, 56.

38. *CAD* I/J 328a, *AHw* 413a.

39. Collon, *Seals*, 35.

stones.[40] It should be noted that NLT adds the colors of the lesser known stones.[41]

One final comment concerns the Hebrew word *zᵉkôkît* (Job 28:17), sometimes translated "glass."[42] It is perhaps cognate with the Akkadian *zakakatu* "glass," "glaze."[43] Large-scale glass-making began ca. 1600 BC.[44] Glass beads were found in Tutankhamun's tomb[45] and 170 glass ingots were found in the Uluburun shipwreck.[46]

From material evidence relating to precious and semiprecious stones we now turn to evidence connected with disease.

40. Harell et al., "Hebrew Gemstones," 1–30. For appendix 4 see pages 129–32.

41. But its "pale green peridot" for *piṭdāh* (17b) and "orange jacinth" for *lešem* (19a) are at variance with evidence presented above. It should also be noted that CEV gives the colors of the Rev 21:19–20 stones in a footnote.

42. BDB 269a, *HALOT* 269b, RSV, NRSV, ESV.

43. *CAD* Z 15b, *AHw* 1503b.

44. Philip, *DANE* 129.

45. Habel, *Job*, 391.

46. Mattingly, *DANE* 307; Konen, "Shipwrecks," 394.

8

"Unclean! Unclean!" Lev 13:45b

The Archaeology of Disease

Bubonic Plague

THE HEBREW TERM *DEBER* (Exod 5:3) is sometimes rendered "bubonic plague,"[1] but since the symptoms of bubonic plague, an inflamed swelling (bubo) in the groin or armpit caused by the flea *Yersina pestis*, are nowhere stated in the Old Testament, it may be better to adopt the more general "plague" or "pestilence."[2] The first undisputed case of bubonic plague was in Egypt in AD 540, followed two years later by the great outbreak in Constantinople which killed some 300,000, perhaps 40 percent of the population.[3]

1. *HALOT* 212a.

2. BDB 184a, *DCH2*, 411a.

3. Procopius (ca. AD 507–55), *History of the Wars*, 2.22.1–23.21; Norwich, *Early Centuries*, 233.

Leprosy

The Hebrew term *ṣāra'at* has traditionally been translated "leprosy." See AV's rendering of Lev 13:9: "When the plague of leprosy is in a man, then he shall be brought to the priest." Modern versions adopt a broader term "infectious skin disease" or the like[4] for *ṣāra'at* and its Greek counterpart λεπρα [lepra]. The term "leprosy" is now used for a specific medical condition known as Hansen's disease (identified by the Norwegian Gerhard Hansen in 1873). However, we should note that the chief diagnostic criteria of white spots on the skin and white hair given in Lev 13:3, 4, 10 do not match those of Hansen's disease. In addition, the absence in Lev 13–14 of any of the classic symptoms of Hansen's disease—loss of sensation of the skin, wasting of fingers and toes, facial nodules and blindness—further invalidates the equation. The main reason for this change in Bible translation is medical rather than archaeological.

Nevertheless there is very limited archaeological evidence in antiquity for Hansen's disease. The earliest known example can be seen in bones found at Karataş in southern Turkey, and generally dated to 2700–2300 BC.[5]

A later example is provided by the skull of a man with bone damage in the upper jaw due to Hansen's disease "leprosy." It was found at a cemetery at Balat in the Dakhleh oasis in Egypt and is dated to ca. 250 BC.[6] Hansen's disease "leprosy" would seem to have been endemic in Egypt and Israel in the first century AD.[7] So the situation in the time of the New Testament would seem to be somewhat different from that of the Old Testament.

From the evidence connected with disease we now turn to a brief consideration of arguably the most significant of all

4. NIV2 has "defiling skin disease."

5. Angel, "Human Skeletal Remains at Karataş," 253–59. This invalidates Hulse's often cited assertion (Hulse, "Nature of Biblical 'Leprosy,'" 88) that Hansen's disease was brought west from India by the soldiers of Alexander the Great (336–23 BC).

6. Dzierzykray-Rogalski, "Paleopathology," 71–74.

7. Zias, *Past and Present of Leprosy*, 262.

archaeological discoveries relevant to the Old Testament—that provided by the Dead Sea Scrolls.

9

"A Lion Shouted" Isa 21:8

How the Dead Sea Scrolls Help Us to Better Understand the Hebrew Bible

THE SCROLLS FOUND IN caves near the Dead Sea[1] date from the third century BC to just before the Roman invasion of the area in AD 68. The collection comprises 670 extrabiblical religious texts and a total of 215 manuscripts of every Old Testament book except Esther and Nehemiah. Although the Dead Sea Scrolls cover some 34 percent of the Old Testament there is only one complete scroll—that of the prophet Isaiah. I have selected several examples where the Isaiah Scroll helps us to better understand the traditional text of the Old Testament, known as the Masoretic Text.

Isa 21:8a

The Masoretic Text of Isa 21:8a reads: "A lion shouted: 'Day after day, my lord, I stand on the watchtower.'" The MT *aryēh* "lion"

1. For details of discovery see 9–10 above.

makes little sense here and should be treated as a scribal error.[2] The Dead Sea Isaiah Scroll reads *hā-rō'eh* "the seer" or "lookout." It is also the reading of the Syriac version. Hence most modern versions read: "The lookout shouted, 'Day after day, my lord, I stand on the watchtower.'"

Isa 33:8b

The Masoretic Text of Isa 33:8b is rendered by NKJV[3] "he has broken the covenant, he has despised the cities." For *'ārîm* "cities" the Dead Sea Isaiah Scroll reads *'ēdîm* "witnesses." Hence NIV, NIV2 "The treaty is broken, its witnesses are despised." The similarity or *d* and *r* in the Hebrew script can be adduced to explain this variant. An alternative meaning of *'ēdîm* "vassal treaty"[4] would parallel well the previous line "the treaty is broken."

Isa 45:2b

The Masoretic Text of Isa 45:2 is rendered by NKJV "and [I] make the crooked places straight." "Crooked places" *wa-h^{a}dûrîm* is of uncertain meaning.[5] Here the Dead Sea Isaiah Scroll reads *he-hārîm* "the mountains" as does the Septuagint. Hence NIV, NIV2 "I . . . will level the mountains."

2. Even AV "And he cried. A lion: My Lord, I stand continually upon the watchtower in the daytime" (NKJV is virtually identical) and NJPS "[Like] a lion he called out: 'On my Lord's lookout I stand ever by day'" try to smooth out this difficulty.

3. The NKJV is a modernization, from 1982, of the AV, which modernizes the language in places, but leaves the text essentially the same. It can be said to represent biblical scholarship before the discovery of the Dead Sea Scrolls.

4. Cf. NJPS footnote. This is based on Aramaic *'dy* (the Old Aramaic Sefire treaty 3 from Syria [Bar-Gayah of KTK with Attar-sumki of Arpad] [ca. 783 BC], 4; Kitchen and Lawrence, *Treaty, Law and Covenant*, 912–13); Akkadian *adû* "treaty" *CAD* A1, 131b, *AHw* 14a; Cohen, *Hapax Legomena*, 42. For discussion of the location of KTK see Lawrence, *Books of Moses*, 55n27.

5. BDB 213a takes it as a passive participle of the verb *hdr* "to swell," i.e., "the swellings."

Isa 49:24b

The Masoretic Text of Isa 49:24b is rendered by NKJV "or captives of the righteous be delivered?" For *ṣaddîq* "righteous" the Dead Sea Isaiah Scroll reads *'ārîṣ* "fierce." Hence NIV, NIV2 "Can . . . captives be rescued from the fierce?" This is also the reading of the Syriac and Vulgate versions.

Isa 53:11a

A more famous example is provided by Isa 53:11a. The Masoretic Text reads the equivalent of: "He will see from the suffering of his soul and be satisfied." However, the preposition *mē*—"from" is often ignored with a translation: "He will see the suffering of his soul and be satisfied." The Dead Sea Isaiah Scroll (and also the Septuagint) however, adds an object *ōr* "light" and thus makes better sense of the frequently ignored *mē*—"Out of the suffering of his soul he will see light and be satisfied."

From this brief look at the Dead Sea Scrolls we now turn to a consideration of how some of the place names of the Bible can be better understood using archaeological evidence.

10

"Woe to Me That I Dwell in Meshek" Ps 120:5

The Archaeology of Places

THERE ARE SEVERAL THOUSAND geographical names mentioned in the Bible. Some are settlements ranging in size from villages and desert oases to large cities. Others are areas or regions, some of which are used to designate kingdoms or political entities. Occasionally an ancient region does not coincide with its modern namesake. "Asia" of the New Testament is a good case in point. However, generally it seems best to translate geographical names by their ancient Hebrew and Greek names, not by their modern equivalents.[1] Archaeological evidence sometimes comes into

1. Thus I would argue for Aram instead of Syria in the Old Testament. For names of cities in Egypt, e.g., Memphis and Thebes, it might be better to follow these Greek-based forms rather than Hebrew Moph (Hos 9:6)/ Noph (Isa 19:13) and No Amon (Nah 3:6) which are not well known. However, I would use Jerusalem, not any Islam-based modern equivalent, which is anachronistic in a biblical context. Locations do not need to be specified unless maps are prepared to accompany a translation. The case of Perath in Jer 13:4 poses a unique problem. Jeremiah is told to go to a place called Perath (so NEB/REB, NIV, NIV2, NJPS, CEV) and bury a linen belt there. This is traditionally taken as "The Euphrates" (also called Perath in Hebrew), but this is approximately 500 km away, so although it is possible that Jeremiah could have made a double

play when attempting to locate geographical names. Here are some representative examples, all of which are to be located outside the modern land of Israel.

Ararat

Ararat, the name given to the resting place of Noah's ark (Gen 8:4), is the Hebrew equivalent of the Assyrian term Urartu, an area comprising much of what is now eastern Turkey. This name is first attested in an inscription of the Assyrian king Shalmaneser I (1273–1244 BC).[2] Ararat is the name now given to that region's highest peak Büyük Ağrı Dağı (5,156 m) and some have claimed wooden remains found on that mountain are those of Noah's ark.[3] Perhaps more significant is that claims of remains of a boat in the Armenian mountains have a long history—the earliest being made by Berossus ca. 275 BC[4] and Abydenus second century AD.[5] It should, however, be noted that Gen 8:4 describes the resting place as *hārê ᵃrārāṭ*—"mountain<u>s</u> of Ararat," suggesting a wider geographical area may be in view. This is certainly the case of "the land of Ararat" mentioned in 2 Kgs 19:37 || Isa 37:38 as the place of escape of the assassins of the Assyrian king Sennacherib (704–681 BC).

The Table of the Nations Gen 10:1–32

The book of Genesis lists many ancient peoples, showing them as descendants of Noah's three sons—Japheth, Ham, and Shem. A number of peoples, listed in Gen 10:2 as descendants of Noah's son Japheth, are discussed briefly below. Particular emphasis is given

---

return journey there, it is much more likely that he went only as far as the Wadi Farah only 5 km NE of his home town of Anathoth, where his own people could easily observe his actions.

2. Grayson *Assyrian Rulers* 1, 183 line 40. Its Urartian equivalent was Biainele. Diakonoff and Kashkai, *Geographical Names*, 94.

3. Hence the growth of so-called "Arkeology."

4. Quoted in Josephus, *Against Apion* 1.130.

5. Jacoby, *Die Fragmente* 3C, 402 §385, 3.5.

initially here to names that can be substantiated in the historical records of Assyria and Babylonia and to their first known occurrence in history.

Gomer

Gomer, perhaps known to the Assyrians as Gamir, was first mentioned in correspondence from crown-prince Sennacherib to his father Sargon (721–05 BC).[6] Sennacherib mentions that an unnamed king of Urartu, perhaps Rusa I (719–14 BC),[7] was defeated in Gamir. Gamir would seem to be located somewhere in Transcaucasia or western Iran,[8] and is sometimes taken as a reference to the Cimmerians of Greek sources[9] who originated on the steppes of modern Ukraine, and who pressed from the rear by the Scythians[10] were eventually defeated at Hubushna (probably Ereğli in the Turkish province of Karaman)[11] in 679 BC by the Assyrian king Esarhaddon.[12]

Magog

Magog may possibly reflect the Akkadian phrase ^{māt}Gugu "land of Gog." Gog may be Gyges, the Greek name of the celebrated king of Lydia in western Turkey, who died in 644 BC,[13] and who

6. Parpola, *Correspondence of Sargon II*, 31 §30, obv.6′; §31, obv.9; 32 §32 obv.12.

7. Specified as Rusa I by Bredow, "Cimmerii," 335.

8. Adalı, *Scourge of God*, 112.

9. Mentioned in Homer, *Odyssey*, 11.14.

10. Barnett, "Urartu," 355. For the Scythians see below 86.

11. Köroğlu and Adalı, *Assyrians*, 292.

12. Borger, *Inschriften Asarhaddons*, 33 §21, 18; 51 episode 8, 3.43–46; 100 §66.23–24; Luckenbill, *ARAB* 2 §§516, 530, 546; Sulimirski and Taylor, "Scythians," 558; the Esarhaddon Chronicle entry for 679 BC mentions a variant Shubuhnu. Grayson, *Chronicles*, 125. Gomer is also mentioned in Ezek 38:6.

13. Prism F of the Assyrian king Ashurbanipal (668–30 BC) reports Gyges still living in 645 BC. Prism A, written in 643/642 BC reports his son Ardys as

is mentioned in the Annals of the Assyrian king Ashurbanipal (668–30 BC).[14]

Madai

The Madai are the Medes from Iran, first attested in the celebrated Assyrian monument the Black Obelisk of Shalmaneser III, which records that in Shalmaneser's 24th regnal year, 834 BC "I went down to the land of Amadāya."[15]

Tubal

Tubal is the area known in Assyrian texts as Tabālu, also first mentioned in the Black Obelisk of Shalmaneser III (858–24 BC), but in a section dealing with his 22nd regnal year, 836 BC.[16] It is probably the area now represented by the modern Turkish provinces of Kayseri, Nevşehir, Niğde, and Aksaray.[17]

Meshek

Meshek are the Mushku, a tribe from what is now central Turkey, first mentioned in the entry of Annals of the Assyrian king Tiglath-pileser I for 1115 BC which records that Tiglath-pileser I

ruling, so it is now proposed that Gyges died in 644 BC, not in 652 BC as earlier proposed. For the date of the end of Ashurbanipal's reign see above 31n43.

14. This would appear to be the latest historical reference latent in the Table of Nations (Gen 10:1–32), an indication perhaps that it was written, or at least underwent its final revision, after this date; see further Lawrence, *Books of Moses*, 36.

15. The Black Obelisk of Shalmaneser III, line 121. Grayson, *Assyrian Rulers* 2, 68; Luckenbill, *ARAB* 1, 206 §579.

16. The Black Obelisk of Shalmaneser III, line 105. Grayson, *Assyrian Rulers* 2, 67; Luckenbill, *ARAB* 1, 206 §581.

17. Starke, "Asia Minor," 124; Aro, "Tabal," 388b; Köroğlu and Adalı, *Assyrians*, 276. It may be known in Urartian as Tap/blane. Diakonoff and Kashkai, *Geographical Names*, 83.

defeated five of kings of the Mushku and an army of 20,000 men.[18] A king named as Mita of Mushku was contemporary with the Assyrian king Sargon II (721–05 BC).[19] Mita is commonly identified with Midas, of Greek sources, the king of Phrygia. For the psalmist (Ps 120:5), Meshek appears to have developed a metaphorical meaning of a far-distant place, similar to our use of Mongolia or Timbuktu: "Woe to me that I dwell in Meshek." Among Japheth's grandsons the following are listed (Gen 10:3).

Ashkenaz

Ashkenaz is perhaps to be equated with the Ishkuzai mentioned in prayers offered to the sun god Shamash during the reign of the Assyrian king Esarhaddon (680–669 BC).[20] After defeating the Ishkuzai,[21] Esarhaddon received a request from their king Bartatua requesting his daughter in marriage.[22] It is unknown whether or not Esarhaddon agreed to this proposal.[23] The Ishkuzai were an Indo-European people from southern Russia, the Scythians of Greek sources.[24] There are possible earlier references to the

18. The Annals of Tiglath-pileser I, 1.62–63. For text see Grayson, *Assyrian Rulers* 1, 14; Luckenbill, *ARAB* 1, 74 §221. The term is also known from Urartian sources. Diakonoff and Kashkai, *Geographical Names*, 59.

19. E.g., Luckenbill, *ARAB* 2, 8 §18; Oppenheim, "Babylonian and Assyrian Historical Texts," 285.

20. Star, I. *Queries*, 40 §35, obv.4; 77 §66, obv.5; 80 §71 rev.3′.

21. Possibly to be dated to 676 BC. Grayson, "Assyria," 128.

22. Star. I, *Queries*, 25 §20, rev. 5–7. Bartatua may be the Protothyes of Herodotus, *Histories*, 1.103.

23. Grayson, "Assyria," 129.

24. Loon, *Urartian Art*, 16, argues that from the start the terms "Cimmerian" and "Scythian" were interchangeable. The only difference seems to have been that the first "Cimmerian" wave entered western Asia along the west side of the Caucasus and operated mostly in what is Turkey, whereas the second "Scythian" wave came in along the east side of the Caucasus and operated what is now Azerbaijan, Iraq, and Syria.

Ishqigulu land in two inscriptions of the Urartian king Argishti (785/780–756 BC).[25]

Togarmah

The name Togarmah, known as Tegarama in Old Assyrian texts,[26] was first found in texts from the Assyrian trading post of Kanesh (Kültepe), near Kayseri in central Turkey, which ceased trading ca. 1780 BC. It is listed in a treaty made by the Hittite king Suppiluliuma I (14th century BC) with Shattiwaza king of Mitanni,[27] and may perhaps be identified with the city called La/ukarma in a hieroglyphic Luwian[28] inscription probably dating from the twelfth century BC from Karahöyük in Elbistan (in the Turkish province of Kahramanmaraş).[29]

As Tagari[immu] it was also mentioned by Shalmaneser III in an account of his campaign for 835 BC.[30] Traditionally Togarmah has been located at Gürün (in the Turkish province of Sivas),[31] but more recently it has been located in the Elbistan plain.[32]

25. Suggested by Loon, *Urartian Art*, 15. Thus (1) an inscription from Kanlıca near Arpaçayı, Kars, eastern Turkey. Payne, *Urartu Kataloğu*, 183. §8.1.7; and (2) an inscription from Ganlidzha near Leninakan in Armenia. See also Diakonoff and Kashkai, *Geographical Names*, 45.

26. Michel and Garelli, *Tablettes*, 1, 2.11; 11.9; 50.7; 198.3; 200.29.

27. The Treaty of Suppiluliuma I with Shattiwaza of Mitanni. Kitchen and Lawrence, *Treaty, Law and Covenant*, 366–69, lines 13, 20, 22. Shattiwaza is also called Mattiwaza or Kurtiwaza in older scholarly literature.

28. Luwian is an Indo-European Anatolian language related to Hittite.

29. Bossert, "Die Göttin Hepat," 320–21; Yamada, "City of Togarma," 223.

30. Statue from Calah (Nimrud) of Shalmaneser III, line 187′. Grayson, *Assyrian Rulers*, 2:80. Note the restoration of the end of the name.

31. Forrer, *Provinzeinteilung*, 75.

32. Yamada, "City of Togarma," 233. See further my article "Anatolia in the Old Testament," 33–36, though some of my observations are modified here.

Tarshish

Tarshish is another of Japheth's grandsons listed in Gen 10:4. The Hebrew place name Tarshish (1 Kgs 10:22) may have been derived from a Phoenician word for "refinery."[33] It is most possibly the Gualdaquivir valley in southern Spain which the Greeks knew as Ταρτεσσος [Tartessos]. An alternative is Sardinia, where an inscription erected by the Phoenicians in ninth century BC bears the name Tarshish.[34] Less likely is the equation of Tarshish with Tarsus in southern Turkey.[35] Perhaps Tarshish also had the connotation of an idealized place, an ancient-world "El Dorado"—a land so far away that it could only be reached by ocean-going ships.[36]

Kittim

Another of Japheth's grandsons listed in Gen 10:4 was Kittim. The Hebrew place name Kittim is derived from Kition in Cyprus.[37] The Septuagint[38] of Dan 11:30 updates this to "the Romans."

Cush

Cush is listed as a son of Noah's son Ham in Gen 10:6. The name Cush had already been used to name the district traversed by the Gihon River, one of the rivers of Paradise (Gen 2:13). The Egyptian

33. Albright, "Early History of Phoenician Colonization," 21; Albright, *Archaeology*, 133–34; Ikeda, "Solomon's Trade in Horses and Chariots," 234n111, *rašāšu* "to melt, to be smelted" *CAD* R 191a, *AHw* 960b "to glow."

34. Albright, "Early History of Phoenician Colonization," 21.

35. Coins from the Persian period read Trz (not Trs).

36. Gordon, "Wine-Dark Sea," 51–52, on Ps 48:7. Craigie, *Psalms 1–50*, 354.

37. NIV renders it "western coastlands."

38. The Septuagint version of Daniel, which exists in only two manuscripts—(1) a 10th-century manuscript from the Chigi collection in the Vatican and (2) Chester Beatty papyrus 967, early 3rd century AD, originally from Aphroditopolis in Egypt—was replaced by the more literal version of Theodotion from Asia Minor, late 2nd century AD.

term *K3z* (sometimes *K3s*) was used from the Middle Kingdom (2116–1795 BC) and onward, for the region sometimes called Nubia.[39] The identification of Cush with "Ethiopia" in AV 2 Kgs 19:9 is misleading, since the modern country with the same name is centered on the Abyssinian highlands which are much further to the southeast. It should be noted in passing that although the New Testament uses the Greek term Αιθιοψ [Aithiops] "Ethiopian" (Acts 8:27),[40] the term refers to what in Roman times was the Kingdom of Meroë.[41]

Caphtor

The Caphtorites are a people listed among the descendants of Noah's son Ham (Gen 10:14). The Hebrew name Caphtor (Deut 2:23) is Crete, known in Akkadian as *Kaptara*, in Ugaritic as *Kptr*, and in Egyptian as *Kfty(w)*. The Philistines are recorded as coming from there (Amos 9:7) and this fits well with their known Aegean origins.

Ophir

Ophir is listed as a great-great grandson of Noah's son Shem (Gen 10:29). Ophir (1 Kgs 10:11) was from where Hiram, king of Tyre, obtained gold for King Solomon (970–930 BC). In Gen 10:26–29 Ophir is linked with Havilah (perhaps Hawlan—the Yemen-Saudi Arabia border area), Sheba (Saba in Yemen), and Hazarmaweth (Hadhramaut). Consequently a gold-bearing area north of Wadi Baysh (Maʿmal area) in western Arabia has been suggested for Ophir.[42] An alternative is Soupara, mentioned in Ptolemy (ca. AD

39. Kitchen, in *LÄ* 3, 887; Kitchen, *IllBD*, 349; *HALOT* 466b "lands of the Nile in S Egypt, meaning Nubia and N Sudan."

40. So BAGD 26a.

41. Polhill, *Acts*, 223. Also Morkot, in *OCD*, 558b. The kingdom of Meroë was located between the fifth and sixth cataracts of the Nile. Lohwasser, "Meroe," 717.

42. Wissmann, "Ophir," 970.

90–168) *Geography* 7.1, some 65 km north of Mumbai, India.[43] Interestingly the phrase "Gold of Ophir" occurs on an ostracon[44] found at Tell Qasile near the mouth of the Yarkon River in modern Israel and dated to the first half of the eighth century BC.[45] This inscription, however, does not help in locating Ophir, but it is evidence for knowledge of the place name in antiquity and its association with gold.

Other Old Testament Area Names

There are many other area names in the Old Testament that are not mentioned in the Table of Nations, but I have selected only a further two.

Sinim

The Hebrew name *Sinîm* (Isa 49:12) has traditionally been taken as the equivalent of Σιναι [Sinai] of Ptolemy (ca. AD 90–168) *Geography* 7.3, namely China.[46] However, if this name is derived from the name of the Ch'in dynasty (221–26 BC) this cannot be contemporary with Isaiah.[47] More modern opinion, bolstered by the reading *Swn* in the Aramaic papyri from Elephantine,[48] and *Swnym* of the Dead Sea Isaiah Scroll, equates the name with Syene, modern Aswan.[49]

43. Renger, "Ophir," 154.

44. An ostracon is an inscribed potsherd.

45. The full inscription reads *zhb 'pr l-Byt Hrn, š* ≡ "Gold of Ophir for Beth Horon, 30 shekels."

46. BDB 696a. See further Bodde, "State and Empire of Ch'in," 20n2.

47. Or even the putative Deutero-Isaiah of supposed postexilic date ca. 520 BC.

48. Cowley, *Aramaic Papyri*, 85, no. 25 line 3.

49. So NIV, NIV2 "Aswan" or ESV "Syene" This was the site of a Jewish temple at the first cataract of the Nile destroyed in 411 BC and mentioned in the Elephantine papyri from Aswan. "These from the land of Syene" would acquire an additional sting, since it would mean acknowledgement of Jerusalem's

India

India is mentioned in many versions as the translation of the Hebrew *Hoddu* in Esth 1:1, but this use is misleading. Hindush of the Old Persian inscriptions approximates to the Indus valley of modern Pakistan, rather than modern India.[50]

Some Cities

Generally speaking, names of cities are less problematic; at least they are confined to a specific location.

The City of Destruction

The Masoretic Text reads the word *heres* in Isa 19:18, thus NIV "one of them will be called the City of Destruction."[51] However, the Dead Sea Isaiah Scroll has a change to *ḥeres* "sun,"[52] thus making a reference to "Heliopolis"—"the city of the sun." It is known that a Jewish temple was established in 162 BC at Leontopolis in the region of Heliopolis by the Jewish refugee high priest Onias IV. It was modeled on the temple in Jerusalem and was destroyed by the Romans[53] (probably in AD 73). The Masoretic reading seems to reflect the Pharisaic understanding of the passage after the destruction of this Egyptian temple.[54]

---

unique status. Baltzer, *Deutero-Isaiah*, 316.

50. Olmstead, *Persian Empire*, 145; Frye, *Heritage of Persia*, 130. The trilingual Behistun inscription (see 8 above) does not include India in list of 23 provinces that "came to Darius" (Old Persian version) and "obeyed Darius" (Babylonian version), therefore India was not part of empire when great rock inscription was made (520–518 BC) but was incorporated shortly afterward since it is mentioned on the tomb of Darius 515 BC.

51. So BDB 249a.

52. *HALOT* 257a. Also the Greek version of Symmachus, RSV, NRSV, NLT, CEV "City of the Sun."

53. Gray, *Isaiah*, 333. Josephus (AD 37/38–ca. 100), *Antiquities*, 13.68, and *Jewish War*, 7.432, reports that this was justified by citing Isa 19:18–19.

54. Vermes, "Bible and Midrash," 224.

Lair, Sepharvaim

In 2 Kgs 19:13 || Isa 37:13 the phrase "the city of Sepharvaim" is often thought to occur in a list of cities conquered by the Assyrians. However, all the other city names are listed without the designation "the city of" and the Hebrew vocalization *lā-'ir* not *lᵉ'ir* shows that it is a place name (not "the city of").[55] Lair is to be identified with Laḫiru mentioned in Assyrian texts and located in the foothills of the Zagros mountains in modern Iraq and also with a place known as *L'r* in the correspondence of Arsames the Persian satrap of Egypt.[56]

Sepharad

An Aramaic inscription found at Sardis, the capital of Lydia in western Turkey, identifies the city as "the citadel of Sepharad."[57] The same term appears in the prophecy of the Hebrew prophet Obadiah. He wrote at an undetermined date, but certainly after the exile of Judah to Babylon in 586 BC, and predicted a resettlement of the Negev region of Israel by exiles from Jerusalem who had been in Sepharad: "The exiles from Jerusalem who are in Sepharad will possess the towns of the Negev" (Obad 20c NIV). Obadiah would thus seem to have exiles from Sardis in mind.[58]

55. So NEB/REB, NJPS. Cogan and Tadmor, *2 Kings*, 225, 235.

56. Driver, *Aramaic Documents*, 21a.

57. The full text of the inscription reads: "On the fifth of Marcheswan, in the tenth year of Artaxerxes, in the citadel of Sepharad." The identity of the Artaxerxes mentioned here would give an exact date, but three Persian kings are known to have had that name. The most likely date is that of Artaxerxes III (358–38 BC). Marcheswan is the month corresponding to October-November.

58. The name Sepharad has given its name to the Sephardic Jews—Jews of Iberian and North African origin.

Two Seas

Finally, I have selected the names of two seas that can be located more precisely using archaeological evidence.

The Red Sea

The term "Red Sea" has become proverbial in English, being found in all English versions[59] following the Septuagint Ερυθρα Θαλασση [Eruthra Thalasse] and the Vulgate *Mari Rubo*, "Red Sea." However, the Hebrew is *yam sûp* "sea of reed" (Exod 10:19)—rushes or some kind of water plant. *Sûp* represents the Egyptian *ṯwf(y)* "papyrus (plant),"[60] which is first attested in the *Onomasticon of Amenemope* (ca. 1180–1100 BC).[61] Such notable scholars as Rashi (1040–1105), Luther (1483–1546), and Calvin (1509–1564) all adopted "Reed Sea."[62] The main obstacle to wider acceptance of "Reed Sea" seems to be the use of the term Ερυθρα Θαλασση [Eruthra Thalasse], specifically "Red Sea" in Acts 7:36 and Heb 11:29 in the New Testament.

The use of the term "Reed Sea" would seem to give a clue as to where the crossing of the sea took place. The Egyptian *ṯwf(y)* is not restricted to "papyrus," but can apply to other marsh plants. Salt-tolerating reeds and rushes called halophytes thrive in salt marsh areas. So it is possible, even probable, that the Israelites passed through one of the lakes in the Isthmus of Suez, most likely the Ballah Lakes, Lake Timsah, or the Bitter Lakes region.[63]

59. The JB is an exception.

60. Erman and Grapow, *WAS*, 5.359.

61. Lambdin, "Egyptian Loan Words," 153.

62. Hoffmeier, *Israel in Egypt*, 205.

63. Hoffmeier, *Israel in Egypt*, 209, 215. The LXX translators may have thought the body of water in question was the northern limits of the Red Sea, thus engaging in considerable speculation and commentary on the Hebrew text. Another factor that may have influenced the LXX's translation of *yam sûp* by Ερυθρα Θαλασση was that Ptolemy II (285–46 BC) was engaged in canal-building efforts through the Isthmus of Suez to the Red Sea. Consequently, the scribes may have projected their knowledge of this area onto the biblical text.

The Adriatic Sea

The Greek term Αδρια [Adria] of Acts 27:27 is rendered "Adriatic."[64] However, the sea between Crete and Sicily, now called the Ionian Sea, can hardly be described as the Adriatic in modern parlance. The Adriatic of the ancients is known to have extended further south than the modern Adriatic Sea.[65]

Hoffmeier, *Israel in Egypt*, 205.

64. BAGD 21b.

65. Ptolemy (ca. AD 90–168), *Geography*, 3.4; 3.15. Bruce, *Acts*, 462.

11

"Faith Is the Title Deed of Things Hoped For" Heb 11:1

The Archaeology of the New Testament

BEFORE CONCLUDING LET US take a further foray into the New Testament. Evidence comes from two different types of document—papyri and inscriptions on stone. Unlike the Old Testament there are far fewer places where modern discoveries have brought about a change of understanding of a New Testament text.[1]

1. Some changes are the result of giving due consideration to internal contextual evidence rather than archaeological discoveries. Take, for example, the well-known example of Luke 2:7 "no room at the inn." NIV2's departure from the traditional "because there was no room for them in the inn" with its "because there was no guest room available for them" is based on Luke's use of the same Greek word καταλυμα to mean "guest room" in 22:11 and the observation that where Luke needs to use a word for "inn" as in 10:34 he uses a different word πανδοχειον.

Papyri from Egypt

One of the most significant discoveries from Egypt was the preservation of a large number of papyri and papyrus fragments dating from the Hellenistic and Roman periods. Many of these texts are letters, legal documents, and receipts, but there are a number of literary texts, some not preserved elsewhere in the manuscript tradition. These texts attest many of the words used in the Greek New Testament. In a few cases they have shed light on the meaning of words and expressions.

Substance or Title Deed Heb 11:1

One such example is Heb 11:1, where the Greek term ὑποστασις [hupostasis] is rendered "substance" by the AV. Oxyrhynchus papyrus 237 (the complaint of a certain Dionysia against her father Chaeremon dated to AD 186) 8.26[2] has led to the suggestion that the statement be translated: "Faith is the title deed of things hoped for."[3]

Stature or Life Matt 6:27

The AV of Matt 6:27 reads: "Which of you by taking thought can add one cubit to his stature?" Many modern versions[4] such as NIV have: "Who of you by worrying can add a single hour to his life?" The change from "stature" to "life" or "span of life"[5] is the result of a study of its use in Classical literature and the papyri from Egypt which show that the Greek word ἡλικια [hēlikia] is normally, not a word for "height" or "stature," but a word for "life,"

2. Grenfell and Hunt, *Oxyrhynchus Papyri* 2, 163, papyrus 237.8.26 reading ταις των ανδρων ὑποστασεσιν "to the title deeds of the men" has led to the following explanation (176) "the whole body of documents bearing on the ownership of a person's property, deposited in the archives, and forming evidence of ownership."

3. MM 660a; BAGD 1047a; Bruce, *Hebrews*, 278.

4. NEB and NASB appear to be the exception.

5. RSV.

"lifespan," or being "under age"[6] as a marriage contract between a certain Sarapion and his would-be bride Thais, dated to AD 127, clearly shows: "The children being brought up by their mother until they come of age."[7] This can also be seen on another example dated to AD 198–201:[8] "If you can claim the assistance due to immature age, the prefect of the province shall decide the case for release." Luke 19:3 is the only New Testament passage in which ἡλικια [hēlikia] definitively means "stature," where it is used of the famously-short Zacchaeus.

The Kingdom of Heaven Is within You Luke 17:21

Jesus' words to the Pharisees: "The kingdom of heaven is within you," recorded in Luke 17:21, are well known. The phrase εντος ὑμων [entos humōn] "within you" may bear another meaning, "at hand" or "within reach."[9] A text dated to AD 102 Oxyrhynchus papyrus 2342, 1.7–8 mentions a woman who keeps a supply of wine "in her own hands" εντος αυτης [entos autēs] "under her own control" ὑπο κλ[ει]δα [hupo kl[ei]da], literally "under (lock and) key."[10]

There are a number of other examples where, although the papyri may not occasion a change of understanding of a word or phrase, they do show that words used in the New Testament text were in use at that time.

The Mat the Paralyzed Man Was Laid On

In Mark 2:4 Mark describes a paralyzed man being lowered through the dismantled roof on a mat. The term he uses for "mat"

6. BAGD 435b.
7. Grenfell and Hunt, *Oxyrhynchus Papyri* 3, 211, papyrus 496.12.
8. Hunt, *Oxyrhynchus Papyri* 7, 148, papyrus 1020.5.
9. So NEB/REB, NLT and ESV footnotes.
10. Lobel and Roberts, *Oxyrhynchus Papyri* 22, 125, papyrus 2342, 7–8.

is κραβαττος [krabattos].[11] The parallel accounts in Matt 9:2 and Luke 5:24 use the words κλινη [klinē] and κλινιδιον [klinidion] "bed" and "little bed" respectively. Mark's choice of word may be to indicate it was a "poor man's bed."[12] It was used in a papyrus dating from AD 103–17.[13]

The Pods the Pigs Ate

Luke (15:16) uses the Greek word κερατια [keratia] of the pods eaten by the prodigal son during his time away from his father. This is the carob or locust-bean tree *Ceratonia siliqua*.[14] The same term occurs in a papyrus dated to AD 78 detailing the accounts of a farm.[15]

Sweat Cloths

In Acts 19:12 Luke describes handkerchiefs and aprons that had touched Paul being taken to heal the sick. The word for "handkerchiefs" is σουδαρια [soudaria]—a loanword from Latin *sudarium* "a cloth for wiping off perspiration."[16] The term also occurs on a third-century papyrus.[17]

11. It was perhaps originally a Macedonian word, borrowed into Latin as *grabat(t)us* (MM 357b; LSh, 820b). Some Greek MSS have κραββατος. The form with—ββ—prevailed in the east, hence modern Greek κρεββατι.

12. BAGD 563b.

13. Kenyon, *Greek Papyri*, 2:265. Papyrus 191.16.

14. BAGD 540b, LS 798a.

15. Kenyon, *Greek Papyri*, 1:189. Papyrus 131*.7.

16. BAGD 934b, LSh 1790a.

17. Kenyon, *Greek Papyri*, 1:110. Papyrus 121.826. It is also a loanword in Mishnaic Hebrew where it is used of the "scarf" waved by the attendant (*ḥazzān*) of the synagogue at Alexandria. The Babylonian Talmud *Sukkah* 51b.25–26. Epstein, *Seder Me'od* 6, 245.

First Installment

In 2 Cor 1:22 Paul comments that God has given the first installment αρραβων [arrabōn] of the Spirit in our hearts. This word has an interesting history, starting off as a loanword from Semitic,[18] it means a "first installment," as shown in a text dated to AD 97 "a report concerning the first installment of the assignment of arable lands."[19] On a late first-century letter a certain Horus writes to his friend Apion about a mouse-catcher named Lampōn: "Regarding Lampōn the mouse-catcher I paid him for you eight drachmae as a down payment [or first installment] in order that he might catch mice while they are with young. Please send me the money."[20] In a later text from the Fayûm,[21] a contract dated to AD 237, a certain Aurelius Asclepiades agrees to hire two dancing girls (ορχηστρια) [orchēstria] from a certain Aurelius Theon. He wants to use them in a village entertainment. Asclepiades has already advanced to Theon a sum of money as a down payment[22] on their promised salary.[23] Αρραβωνα [Arrabōna] eventually came to mean "engagement (ring)" in modern Greek.[24]

Parchments

In 2 Tim 4:13 Paul, writing from prison in Rome, instructs Timothy to bring him the books and especially the parchments that he had left behind at Troas. The term for parchment is μεμβρανα [membrana]—animal skins cleaned and impregnated with

18. Cf. Hebrew *'ērābôn* BDB 786b. For the verb *'rb* see Gen 38:17 "to give in pledge."

19. Kenyon, *Greek Papyri*, 2:20. Papyrus 143.13.

20. Grenfell and Hunt, *Oxyrhynchus Papyri* 2, 301. Papyrus 299.2–4.

21. The Fayûm is the largest oasis in Egypt.

22. Greek ὑπερ αραβωνος.

23. Grenfell and Hunt, *New Classical Fragments* 2, 67.17.

24. Pring, *Dictionary*, 28a. δαχτυλιδι αρραβωνα (Demotic form = "engagement ring").

lime—another loanword from Latin,[25] which may specifically refer to sheets of parchment fastened together in a notebook.[26] The word also is used in a papyrus dating from ca. AD 400.[27]

The Chief Shepherd

1 Pet 5:4 has the word αρχιποιμην [archipoimēn] "chief shepherd,"[28] a word which has turned up on a wooden label that once hung around the neck of a mummy from Roman Egypt.[29] This was a word that was once considered to be fabricated by the New Testament's writers—an example of what could be called "Christianese." However, archaeology has demonstrated that the New Testament was not written in an in-house lingo, but in words that were in common use at the time.

Inscriptions Approximately Contemporary to the New Testament

In a number of cases inscriptions carved on stone approximately contemporary to the New Testament confirm details of the New Testament text.

The Politarchēs at Thessalonica

One of the features of government in the Roman Empire is that local officials in various regions had their own distinctive titles. In Acts Luke always refers to each local official by his correct title. For example he uses the term πολιταρχης [politarchēs] (city ruler) in Acts 17:8 to describe the officials of Thessalonica. In a

25. BAGD 629a, LSh 1129a2B.
26. Millard, *Reading and Writing*, 63.
27. Hunt, *Oxyrhynchus Papyri* 17, 275. Papyrus 2156.9.
28. BAGD 139b.
29. Deissmann, *Light from the East*, 99–100.

second-century AD inscription from the Vardar Gate at Thessalonica the term πολιταρχης [politarchēs] is used.[30]

The Asiarchēs in Ephesus

In Acts 19:43 Luke uses the term Ασιαρχης [Asiarchēs] in relation to the officials at Ephesus, where an inscription from the Scholastika baths at Ephesus mentions "*Po[blios] Aelios Martiales, the Asiarch*."[31] The same term Ασιαρχης [Asiarchēs] also occurs on an inscription from the theater at nearby Miletus; on an inscription from the agora at Smyrna (modern İzmir) honoring Julius Menkles Diophatos the chief priest of province of Asia, AD 200–250; and on the early third-century AD sarcophagus from Hierapolis of a certain Guthios Pyrrhos.

The Prōtos at Malta

In Acts 28 Luke describes Paul's wintering in Malta. There he encounters Publius, the island's chief official (28:7), called in Greek πρωτος [prōtos], literally "first." The same term occurs on a Greek inscription found on the island: "First of the Maltese and fathers."[32]

The "Meat Market" at Corinth

In 1 Cor 10:25 Paul mentions the meat market at Corinth: "Eat anything sold in the meat market without raising questions of conscience" (NIV). Here the term for "meat market" is μακελλον [makellon].[33] Interestingly the same word occurs in a Latin

30. *IG* 10, 49 §126; Bruce, *Paul*, 223; Bruce, *Acts*, 326; Yamauchi, *Stones and Scriptures*, 114.

31. Engelmann, Knibbe and Merkelbach, *Inschriften von Ephesos*3, 20 §621A; Yamauchi, *Stones and Scriptures*, 118.

32. *IG* 14, 421 §601; Bruce, *Acts*, 472.

33. BAGD 611b. It is not a Latin loanword (as is sometimes claimed) since it occurs in a Greek inscription from Epidaurus in Greece ca. 400 BC.

inscription dating from the early first century AD, found near the Lechaion road north of the agora[34] in Corinth: "Quintus Cornelius Secundus, son of . . . and his wife Maecia . . . [built] the meat market . . . long with . . . and a fish market."[35]

With our brief look at the New Testament our survey of archaeology and its contribution to Bible translation is now complete. We now offer a conclusion.

34. The agora was the market place of an ancient Greek city.

35. Kent, *Corinth* 8/3, 127–28.

12

Conclusion

IN 1620, AS A group of the so-called Pilgrim Fathers were about to leave Delfshaven in the Netherlands aboard *The Speedwell* for New England, their pastor John Robinson challenged them with these words: "The Lord has more truth yet to break forth out of His Holy Word."[1] It is beyond the scope of this book to comment further on Robinson's challenge, but he would doubtless be surprised to learn that in the succeeding centuries evidence derived from the ground—what we now call "archaeology"—would at least have shed some more light on that Holy Word.[2]

I hope I have been able to show how, in the last two hundred years or so, many important archaeological discoveries relating to the Bible text have been made. Some of these discoveries have changed our understanding of the biblical text, and some of these discoveries are reflected in some modern Bible translations.[3]

Translation teams, however, tend to want to perpetuate tradition and can be resistant to change. Of course, many just do not

1. John Robinson in Thomas, *Golden Treasury*, 39.

2. A thought recently offered, perhaps *in extremis*, by Thomas Davis: "Theologians do not like it when I say it, but the only way we ever learn anything new about the Bible is through archaeology," in *Artifax* 34/2 (2019) 7b.

3. It is evidently more true in connection with the Old Testament than with the New.

know of modern archaeological discoveries, or, if they do, fail to understand how such discoveries might impact the world of Bible translation. I hope that this book has served to bring you more up to date in certain areas and has explained some of the changes made in English Bible translation made over the last hundred years or so. It is, of course, impossible to predict what archaeological discoveries will be made in the coming years, but I would urge all Bible teachers, translators, and scholars to at least try to keep abreast of them to further their understanding of the biblical text.

Appendix 1

Musical Instruments

Reference	Heb. Name	Eng. Name	Archaeological Evidence	Represented in Art
Gen 4:21	*kinnôr*	lyre	9 lyres at Royal Cemetery of Ur (ca. 2500 BC).	Lyres shown on "Standard of Ur" (ca. 2500 BC); on a fresco from the tomb of Khnumhotep at Beni Hasan in Egypt, ca. 1900 BC; on an ivory tablet from Megiddo, Israel, 13th C BC; on a seal from Tel Batash, Israel, 12th c. BC. Lyre players shown on jars from Megiddo, 1150–1000 BC and from Kuntillet ʿAjrud in northern Sinai, ca. 800 BC; on a stone relief, from Zincirli, south-east Turkey, ca. 730 BC.

Appendix 1

Reference	Heb. Name	Eng. Name	Archaeological Evidence	Represented in Art
1 Sam 10:5	*nebel*	harp ?	3 harps at Royal Cemetery of Ur. Egyptian harp from the 18th–19th Dynasties (1540–1186 BC).	Harpists shown on an incised stone from Megiddo, in Israel, ca. 3200–3000 BC; on a stone relief from Bismaya, Iraq, early 3rd millennium BC; on a tomb painting from Thebes, reign of Tuthmosis IV (1401–1391 BC).
Gen 4:21	*`ûgāb*	flute	Horizontal flute at Megiddo, Israel. 3rd millennium BC. 11 other ancient flutes found in Israel—latest from En-Gedi 7th–6th C. BC.	Vertical flute shown on a seal from the Old Akkadian period (2334–2193 BC).

Reference	Heb. Name	Eng. Name	Archaeological Evidence	Represented in Art
1 Sam 10:5	*ḥālîl*	pipe	Double pipe from Nippur, Iraq and 11 examples from ancient Israel.	Double pipe shown on an ivory plaque from Tell el-Far'ah (South), Israel, 14th C. BC; on a faience figurine from Tell el-Far'ah (North), Israel; on a bronze tripod from Megiddo, Israel 12th–10th C. BC; on a clay figurine from Akzib, Israel 8th–6th C. BC; on a stone relief of the Assyrian king Ashurbanipal (668–30 BC).
Gen 31:27	*tōp*	frame-drum		Frame-drum shown on Sumerian seals 2700–2500 BC; on Babylonian figurines, ca. 2000 BC; on an ivory box from Nimrud, Iraq, ca. 800 BC; on a clay figurine from Akzib, Israel 8th–6th C. BC; on a stone relief from Zincirli, south-east Turkey, ca. 730 BC.

Appendix 1

Reference	Heb. Name	Eng. Name	Archaeological Evidence	Represented in Art
Exod 28:33	*pa῾amôn*	bell	Bells 20–40 cm in diameter, from the early 1st millennium BC have been found in Megiddo, Akzib, and Ziklag, Israel and also in Mesopotamia, Egypt.	Bells shown on the attire of a Syrian emissary, on a fresco from an Egyptian tomb Tuthmosis III (1479–1425 BC). Assyrian stone reliefs (early 1st millennium BC) regularly show horses with bells around their necks.
Num 10:2	*ḥaṣōṣerāh*	trumpet	Silver and bronze trumpets from tomb of Tutankhamun (1336–1327 BC) and from Uluburun shipwreck (late 14th C. BC).	Trumpet shown on a stone relief from Amarna of Akhenaten (1352–1336 BC); on a potsherd from Beth-Shan in Israel, 14th C. BC.
2 Sam 6:5	*mena῾an῾îm*	sistrum	Sistrum from Bethel, and Egypt ca. 850 BC. 70+ examples of clay rattles from ancient Israel.	Sistrum shown on Sumerian seal, ca. 2500 BC.
1 Sam 18:6	*šālîšîm*	sistrum	See above.	See above.

Reference	Heb. Name	Eng. Name	Archaeological Evidence	Represented in Art
2 Sam 6:5	*ṣelṣelîm*	cym-bals	Several cymbals from Egypt after 850 BC; west Iran 9th–7th C BC. 28+ examples from ancient Israel.	Cymbals shown in Middle Assyrian (ca. 1350–1000) art. A Babylonian plaque, ca. 700–600 BC, shows lady cymbalist.
1 Chr 13:8	*meṣiltayim*	cym-bals	See above.	See above.
	Aramaic Name			
Dan 3:5c	*qayterôs* Gk. κιθαρα	lyre/ lute	For lyre, see above.	For lyre see above.
Dan 3:5d	*sabka* Gk. σαμβυκη	harp	See above.	See above.
Dan 3:5e	*pesanṭērîn* Gk. ψαλτηριον	psal-tery/ harp	For harp, see above.	For harp see above.
Dan 3:5f	*supōnyā* Gk. τυμπανον	kettle drum		Large drums shown in Sumerian art, ca. 2500 BC.

Appendix 2

Plants and Trees

Reference	Name	Eng. Name	Scientific Name	Archaeological Evidence	Represented in Art	Textual Evidence
Num 11:5	*qiššuāh*	musk-melon	*Cucum ismelo* var. chate	≠ cucumber. Seeds found in Predynastic Egypt 3500 BC.	Shown on several Egyptian tomb paintings and on a piece of linen.	Akk. *qiššû* from Old Babylonian period (1894–1595 BC) onward.
Num 11:5	*abaṭṭiaḥ*	water-melon	*Citrullus vulgaris*	Seeds dating from Eg.12th Dynasty (1973–1795 BC). Baskets of seeds in Tutankhamun's (1336–1327 BC) tomb.		Eg. *bdw-k3*
Num 11:5	*ḥāṣîr*	leek	*Allium porrum*	Two dried specimens found in Eg. tombs.	Shown on wall carvings in Egyptian tombs.	Akk. *karašu* from Sin-muballit (1812–1793 BC) of Babylon.
Num 11:5	*bāṣāl*	onion	*Allium cepa*	Well-preserved onions from Egyptian 18th D (1540–295 BC), later bulbs placed in mummies.	Shown on wall carvings in the pyramids of Unas (2392–2362 BC) and Pepi II (2287–2193 BC).	
Num 11:5	*šûm*	garlic	*Allium sativum*	Numerous garlic bulbs, some with leaves, in Tutankhamun's tomb.		from Old Akkadian period (2334–2193 BC) onward.

Reference	Name	Eng. Name	Scientific Name	Archaeological Evidence	Represented in Art	Textual Evidence
2 Sam 17:28	*pôl*	broad bean	*Vicia faba*	At Jericho 5000–4000 BC and in Egyptian 5th D (2515–2362 BC) burials.		
Gen 25:34	*`adāšāh*	lentil	*Lens culinaris*	At Mureybit and Tell Abu Hureyra in north Syria 9200–7500 BC. Also in Tutankhamun's tomb.		
Isa 30:24	*ḥāmîṣ*	chick pea	*Cicer arietinum*	Found in EB/MB ca. 2000 BC at Lachish, and Arad in Israel, at Jericho and also in Tutankhamun's tomb.		
Exod 9:32	*kussemet*	emmer wheat	*Triticum turgidum*	Principal wheat from the beginning of agriculture 8th–7th millennia BC in the Near East. Emmer was found in a model granary in Tutankhamun's tomb.		
Isa 29:25	*śôrāh*	millet	*Panicum miliaceum*	Tell Deir Alla in Jordan (ca. 1200–500 BC); Nimrud, Iraq, 7th C BC.		

Reference	Name	Eng. Name	Scientific Name	Archaeological Evidence	Represented in Art	Textual Evidence
Ezek 4:9	*dōḥan*	millet		See above.		In Babylonia from Middle Babylonian period (1595–1171 BC) onward.
Ezek 27:19	*pannag*	millet ?		See above.		
Exod 16:31	*gad*	coriander	*Coriandrum sativum*	Coriander seeds were found in Tutankhamun's tomb and at Uluburun shipwreck.		Mentioned in Eg. medical Papyrus Ebers ca. 1550 BC.
Isa 28:25	*kammōn*	cumin	*Cuminum cyminum*	A basket full of cumin was included in the burial of an architect of Amenophis III (1392–1354 BC).		Akk. *kamūnu* Old Akkadian period (2334–2193 BC) onward. Myc. Gr. *kumino*
Isa 28:25	*qeṣaḥ*	black cumin	*Nigella sativa*	Seeds found in Tutankhamun's tomb, the Uluburun shipwreck and at En-Gedi in Israel.		

Reference	Name	Eng. Name	Scientific Name	Archaeological Evidence	Represented in Art	Textual Evidence
Matt 23:23	ανηθον	dill	*Anethum graveo-lens*	Several twigs of dill were found in the tomb of Amenophis II (1428–1402 BC). ≠ anise (AV) *Pimpinella anisa* unlikely to have been grown in Palestine in NT times.		
Gen 40:9 Gen 9:21	*gepen* *yayin*	vine/ wine	*Vitis vinifera*	Grape pips in a carbonized or petrified state have been found at a number of southern Caucasus Neolithic sites. Carbonized grape pips from the Egyptian 1st D (3100–2850 BC) found in tombs at Abydos. Raisins found at 3rd D Zoser's (2691–2672 BC) Step Pyramid at Saqqara. Shriveled grapes and pips were found in Tutankhamun's tomb.		Heb. *yayin* from proto-Indo-European **woino from* √**w(e)i* "to weave," "to plait," "to twist" or Georgian *ğvino* "wine."

Reference	Name	Eng. Name	Scientific Name	Archaeological Evidence	Represented in Art	Textual Evidence
Exod 28:33	*rimmôn*	pomegranate	*Punica granatum*	Whole pomegranates found in the Uluburun shipwreck.	Shown on a wall painting from tomb at Thebes Ramesside period (1295–1070 BC)	
Prov 25:11	*tappûaḥ*	apple	*Malus pumila*	Small apples were found among the offerings deposited in a tomb in the Royal Cemetery of Ur(ca. 2500 BC). Carbonized apples at Kadesh Barnea, Sinai in a 9th C BC context. ≠ "apricot" which only reached the Roman world in AD 63.		Eg. *tpḥ*. Papyrus of Eg. king Ramesses II (1279–1213 BC) discloses that the fields of the Delta were full of apples.
Gen 30:37	*lûz*	almond	*Amygdalus communis*	≠ "hazel" AV. Found at Tutankhamun's tomb and the Uluburun shipwreck.		

Reference	Name	Eng. Name	Scientific Name	Archaeological Evidence	Represented in Art	Textual Evidence
Gen 43:11	*boṭnāh*	terebinth	*Pistacia palaestina*	*Pistacia vera* originated in Central Asia and was only introduced into the Near East at the time of Alexander the Great (336–323 BC), but shells or related species *Pistacia palaestina/ terebinthus* found in EB (ca. 3000 BC) Lachish, Timna, and Arad in Israel, Mostagedda and Memphis in Egypt and Tell Iktanu in Jordan. Resin from the above was found in the Uluburun shipwreck.		An 18th C tablet from Nippur in Mesopotamia mentions that Ishme Dagan king of Assyria sent pistachio nuts to his brother who was ruling as a king of Mari (in Syria).
Judg 9:15	*erez*	cedar	*Cedrus libani*	Cedar found in the ship of Eg. king Cheops (2593–2570 BC) at Giza, coffin of Queen Meritamon (1450–1425 BC) from Deir el-Bahri and at Tutankhamun's tomb. May include *Abies cilicia* (Cilician fir) and other conifers.		
Lev 14:4	*erez*	other conifer		See above.		

Reference	Name	Eng. Name	Scientific Name	Archaeological Evidence	Represented in Art	Textual Evidence
Gen 30:37	*`ermôn*	plane	*Platanus orientalis*	≠ chesnut (sic) AV		
Gen 25:5	*šiṭṭîm*	acacia	*Acacia nilotica*	A 3 m long plank that may be acacia has been found at Mersa/Wadi Gawasis, on the Red Sea coast of Egypt.		Eg. *šnḏ.(t)* from end of 5th D (2362 BC) onward.
Lev 23:40	*`arābāh*	Euphrates poplar/willow		≠ weeping willow *Salix babylonica* (ex. China). Ps 137:1 = *Populus euphratica*. Species of willow elsewhere.		
1 Kgs 10:11	*almug*	Red sandalwood ?	*Pterocarpus santolinus*	≠ sandalwood		Akk. *elemakku(m) / elemaggu(m)* Old Babylonian (1894–1595 BC) onward. Ug. *almg*. (to ca. 1180 BC). Identification uncertain.

Reference	Name	Eng. Name	Scientific Name	Archaeological Evidence	Represented in Art	Textual Evidence
2 Chr 2:7	*algum*	Grecian juniper ?	*Juniperus excelsa*	Some equate with *almug* above, others treat it as a separate tree.		
Ezek 27:15	*hābenîm*	ebony	*Dalbergia melanoxylon*	= African blackwood. Found in Tutankhamun's tomb and the Uluburun shipwreck.		Eg. *hbny* of African origin
Rev 18:12	θυινος	citron (should not be confused with trees of the citrus family)	*Callitris quadrivalvis / Tetraclinis articulata*			Used to make expensive, long-lasting tables. Pliny *Natural History* 13.92.
Exod 9:31	*pištāh*	flax	*Linum usitatissimum*			Gezer calendar ca. 925 BC.

Reference	Name	Eng. Name	Scientific Name	Archaeological Evidence	Represented in Art	Textual Evidence
Gen 41:42	*šeš*	fine linen		Linen kilt and sash and a large shroud from "Cave of the Warrior" ca. 4000 BC near Jericho. Remains of flax seeds from El Omari in Egypt ca. 3200 BC, Textiles made from flax were common in Egypt from the Old Kingdom (2700–2136 BC) onward. Flax seeds and linen were found in Tutankhamun's tomb. Fragments of linen found at Çatal Hüyük in central Turkey ca. 6000 BC and from the Fayûm A culture in Egypt ca. 4000 BC.	Weaving of flax is recorded on the Egyptian 12th D (1973–1795 BC) Beni-Hasan grave paintings. The harvesting of flax is shown on an 18th D (1540–1295 BC) tomb.	*Eg. šš* Middle Kingdom (2116–1795 BC) onward.

Reference	Name	Eng. Name	Scientific Name	Archaeological Evidence	Represented in Art	Textual Evidence
1 Chr 4:21	*bûṣ*	fine linen		See above	See above	Later replaced by Akk. *būṣu* reign of Shalmaneser III (858–24 BC) onward.
Esth 1:6	*karpas*	cotton	*Gossypium herbaceum*	Fragments of cotton textiles and strings found at Mohenjo-Daro in the Indus Valley of Pakistan dating to ca. 1800 BC.		Skt. *karpâsa*. Assyrian king Sennacherib ca. 694 BC mentions "trees that bear wool." Herodotus (5th c. BC) *Histories* 3.106.
Jonah 4:6	*qiyqāyôn*	castor-oil plant	*Ricinus communis*			Eg. *kaka* = Gr κικι Herodotus *Histories* 2.94.
Gen 35:27	*lōṭ*	ladanum	*Cistus laurifolius* or *creticus*			Herodotus *Histories* 3.107, 112.

Reference	Name	Eng. Name	Scientific Name	Archaeological Evidence	Represented in Art	Textual Evidence
Song 4:14	*karkōm*	saffron	*Crocus sativus*		Saffron gathering shown on the walls of a Minoan building on Thera, Greece destroyed by volcanic eruption 17th–16th C. BC.	
Gen 41:2	*āḥû*	rushes				Eg. *3ḥ(w)*—ending *-u* shows possible Old Kingdom (2700–2136 BC) borrowing.

Appendix 3

Animals and Birds

Reference	Heb. name	Eng. name	Scientific name	Archaeological evidence	Textual evidence
Num 23:22	*rᵉēm*	wild ox	*Bos primigenius*	Shown on Lascaux cave paintings, France and a fresco from Çatal Hüyük in central Turkey.	Tuthmosis III (1479–1425 BC) claimed to have killed 75 out of a herd of 176 wild oxen. Ramesses III (1184–1153 BC) hunted wild oxen in Gezira, Sudan, but these might be Cape buffalo *Syncerus caffer*, mummies of which have been found in Egypt.
1 Kgs 10:22	*tukkîm*	baboon	*Papio cynocephalus* and *Papio hamadryas*	Queen Hatshepsut (1479–1457 BC)'s temple reliefs from Deir el-Bahri depict her trading expedition to Punt, showing baboons living there.	Eg. *ky* = "baboon."

Reference	Heb. name	Eng. name	Scientific name	Archaeological evidence	Textual evidence
Job 38:36	*sekwî*	rooster/ chicken	*Gallus gallus*	Chickens domesticated in Indus river valley, Pakistan by 2000 BC. Chickens on a silver bowl from Tell Basta (Bubastis) in Egypt late 19th D (1295–1186 BC) or early 20th D (1186–1070 BC). Seal of Jaazaniah (ca. 600 BC) from Tell en-Nasbeh shows a fighting rooster. Chicken egg shells from the City of David in Jerusalem ca. 600 BC.	Annals of Tuthmosis III from Karnak records "four birds which lay every day."
Prov 30:31	*zarzîr*	rooster		See above	
1 Kgs 4:23	*barburîm* *ᵃbûsîm*	fattened birds = chickens or geese?		For chickens see above. Force-fed geese shown on Egyptian tomb painting ca. 2500 BC.	
Job 38:36	*ṭuḥāh*	ibis??	*Threskiornis aethiopica*		Eg. *ḏḥwty* = "sacred ibis."

Reference	Heb. name	Eng. name	Scientific name	Archaeological evidence	Textual evidence
Lev 11:15	*`ōrēb*	crow/raven	*Corvus corone/ Corvus corax*		Akk. *āribu* "raven."
Lev 11:18	*rāḥām*	carrion vulture	*Vultur percnop-terus*		Ar. *raḥamu* "carrion vulture."
Lev 11:13	*nešer*	eagle/vulture	several species		Ug. *nšr* and Arabic *nisr* "eagle" also = (Griffon) vulture *Gyps fulvus*.
Lev 11:17	*yanšûp*	kind of owl ?	*Asio otus*		Akk. *enšup/bu* uncertain.
Lev 11:19	*anāpāh*	heron	several species		Akk. *anpatu* uncertain.
Lev 11:19	*dûkîpat*	hoopoe	*Upopa epops*		Eg. *qwqwpt/d* and Coptic *kouk-ouphat* "hoopoe."
Lev 11:29	*`akbār*	jerboa	*Jerboa jaculus*		Akk. *akbaru* "jerboa."

Reference	Heb. name	Eng. name	Scientific name	Archaeological evidence	Textual evidence
Lev 11:29	*ṣāb*	lizard			Ar. *ḏubb* or *ḏabb*"lizard."
Lev 11:30	*ḥōmeṭ*				Akk. *ḫulmiṭṭu* "snake" or "lizard."
Lev 11:30	*tinšemet*				Akk. *tašlamtu* "a type of lizard."
Exod 25:4	*tekēlet*	type of shellfish, producing blue purple dye	*Murex brandaris*	Large heaps of discarded shells of found at Shiqmona near Haifa in Israel, Sarepta in Lebanon, and Ugarit in Syria.	
Exod 24:4	*argāmān*	type of shellfish, producing red purple dye	*Murex trunculus*	Large heaps of discarded shells of found at Shiqmona near Haifa in Israel, Sarepta in Lebanon, and Ugarit in Syria.	Akk. *argamannu*. Hit. *arg/kam-man* originally meant "tribute," since "purple dyed stuffs" were often given as tribute by the inhabitants of the Mediterranean coast.

Reference	Heb. name	Eng. name	Scientific name	Archaeological evidence	Textual evidence
Ezek 16:10	*mešî*	silk	*Pachypasa otus*	Fragments of silk textiles, dating from ca. 750 BC have been found near Van in eastern Turkey, and threads from the Chinese silkworm *Bombyx mori* have been found in Athens in a grave dated to the late 5th c. BC.	Aristotle (384–22 BC) *History of Animals* 551b16.
Exod 25:5	*taḥaš*	dugong /fine leather	*Helicore helicore*	≠ "badger" AV. "porpoise" (NASB) and "dolphin" (NJPS) unlikely.	Arabic *tuḥas* "dugong" = "sea cow." Eg. *ṯḥś* "leather NIV2 "durable leather," NRSV "fine leather."
Exod 30:34	*šeḥēlet*	traditionally onycha (following LXX)			More likely is identification with Akk. *šeḫlātu*, attested in Mari in Syria in the early second millennium BC, a "foodstuff" or "vegetable" or with Ug. *šḥlt* "a certain vegetable." Hit. *zaḫḫeli* and Akk. *sahlû*, *sahlûtu* "cress."

Appendix 4

Precious Stones in Exod 28

Exod 28	Heb. Name	NIV / NIV2	Other English Versions (where appropriate)	Archaeological Evidence	Textual / Lexical Evidence	Harrell, Hoffmeier and Williams[1]
17a	*ōdem*	ruby => carnelian		Carnelian from Royal Cemetery of Ur and the Uluburun shipwreck.	√*'dm* "to be red."	A reddish stone, probably carnelian.
17b	*piṭdāh*	topaz => chrysolite		Haematite common in first 4 centuries of 2nd millennium.	≠ Skt. *pita* "yellow" Eg. *p3ddt* haematite.	Probably the submetallic variety of haematite = red iron ore.
17c	*bāreqet*	beryl	emerald (NASB, JPS, NLT)	Emerald unknown.	≠ Skt. *markata* "emerald"= Akk. *burallu* name of a stone, but identity not known.	A greenish stone, probably serpentinite, but possibly green jasper.
18a	*nōpek*	turquoise		Turquoise production stops at end of New Kingdom 1070 BC.	Eg. *mfk(3.t)* "turquoise."	Turquoise.

1 Harell, "Hebrew Gemstones in the Old Testament," 1–52.

Exod 28	Heb. Name	NIV / NIV2	Other English Versions (where appropriate)	Archaeological Evidence	Textual / Lexical Evidence	Harrell, Hoffmeier and Williams[1]
18b	*sappîr*	sapphire => lapis lazuli	lapis lazuli (NLT)	Sapphire unknown. Lapis lazuli from Badakshan (Afghanistan) found at Royal Cemetery of Ur and Tod treasure of Egyptian king Amenemhat II (1917–1882 BC). In cache of objects found at Thebes in Greece (14th C. BC).	≠ Skt. *sanipriya* "sapphire."	Lapis lazuli.
18c	*yāhalōm*	emerald	diamond (NASB, RSV, ESV, CEV) moonstone (NRSV, NLT)	Diamond (= moonstone) unknown.	Diamond unknown until Manilius's (1st C AD) *Astronomicon* 4.926. = Akk. *ḫulālu*, but identity not known.	Perhaps milky quartz or sapphirine chalcedony.

Exod 28	Heb. Name	NIV / NIV2	Other English Versions (where appropriate)	Archaeological Evidence	Textual / Lexical Evidence	Harrell, Hoffmeier and Williams[1]
19a	*lešem*	jacinth		Green feldspar beads found in Tutankhamun's tomb.	Eg. *nšm.t* "white-blue or green feldspar" mentioned by Tuthmosis III (1479–1425 BC).	A greenish stone, probably amazonite = green feldspar.
19b	*šebô*	agate		Found at the Royal Cemetery of Ur and the Uluburun shipwreck.	Akk. *šubû* described as *arqu* (yellow/green) and *sāmu* (red/brown)	Probably micro-crystalline quartz and most likely banded agate.
19c	*aḥlāmāh*	amethyst		Brought to Egypt from Nubia, D 18 (1540 BC) onwards.	Eg. *ḫnm.(t)* "red jasper" >African origin?	A reddish stone, probably red jasper.
20a	*taršîš*	chrysolite => topaz	Most EVV beryl			Probably amber, but possibly the specularite variety of hematite.

Exod 28	Heb. Name	NIV / NIV2	Other English Versions (where appropriate)	Archaeological Evidence	Textual / Lexical Evidence	Harrell, Hoffmeier and Williams[1]
20b	*šōham*	onyx			Akk. *sāmtu/sāmu* = "carnelian"?	Probably either amethyst or the sardonyx variety of agate.
20c	*yašpēh*	jasper			Akk. *(j)ašpû*> possibly of Hurrian (eastern Turkey) origin. Mentioned in Amarna letter of Tushratta of Mitanni to Amenophis III (1391–1353 BC) of Egypt.	Probably multi-colored, patterned agate or jasper.

Abbreviations

Akk.	Akkadian
Ar.	Arabic
C	century
D	dynasty
EB	Early Bronze
Eg.	Egyptian
Gk.	Greek
Heb.	Hebrew
Hit.	Hittite
MB	Middle Bronze
Myc. Gr.	Mycenaean Greek
Skt.	Sanskrit
Ug.	Ugaritic

Bibliography

Adalı, S. F. *The Scourge of God: The Umman-manda and Its Significance in the First Millennium BC*. State Archives of Assyria 20. Helsinki: Helsinki University Press, 2011.

Albright, W. F. *Archaeology and Religion of Israel*. 3rd ed. Baltimore: Johns Hopkins University Press, 1953.

———. "New Light on the Early History of Phoenician Colonization." *BASOR* 83 (1941) 14–22.

———. "Palestinian Inscriptions." In *ANET*, 320–322.

———. "Some Important Recent Discoveries: Alphabetic Origins and the Idrimi Statue." *BASOR* 118 (1950) 11–20.

Allen, R. B. "Numbers." In *EBC* 2:657–1008.

Angel, J. L. "Human Skeletal Remains at Karataş." *AJA* 74 (1970) 253–59.

Anonymous. *Fauna and Flora of the Bible*. 2nd ed. New York: United Bible Societies, 1980.

Aro, S. "Tabal." In *RLA*, 13:388–91.

Austel, H. J. "shēsh." In *TWOT*, 2:959, §2473.

Baerg, H. J. *Complete Illustrated Guide: Bible Plants and Animals*. Vol. 3, *Plants*. Washington DC: Review & Herald, 1989.

Baltzer, K. *Deutero-Isaiah*. Hermeneia. Minneapolis: Fortress, 2001.

Barker, K. L., ed. *NIV Study Bible*. Grand Rapids: Zondervan, 1985.

Barnett, R. D. "Urartu." In *CAH*, 3/1:314–71.

Ben Yehuda, E. *Pocket English-Hebrew, Hebrew-English Dictionary*. New York: Pocket, 1964.

Bienkowski, P. "Ivory Carving." In *DANE*, 158.

Blades, J. *Percussion Instruments and Their History*. London: Faber, 1975.

Bodde, D. "The State and Empire of Ch'in." In *CHC*, 1:20–102.

Bodenheimer, F. S. *Animal and Man in Bible Lands*. Leiden: Brill, 1960.

Borger, R. *Die Inschriften Asarhaddons Königs von Assyerien*. Graz: 1956.

Bossert, H. T. "Die Göttin Hepat in den Hieroglyphen-Hethitischen Texten." *Belleten* 15 (1951) 315–23.

Braun, J. *Music in Ancient Israel/Palestine*. Grand Rapids: Eerdmans, 2002.

Braun, T. F. R. G. "The Greeks in the Near East." In *CAH*, 3/3:1–31.

Bredow, I. von. "Cimmerii." In *BEAW*, 3:335–37.
Bruce, F. F. *Acts*. London: Tyndale, 1951.
———. *The Epistle to the Hebrews*. New London Commentary Series. London: Marshall, Morgan & Scott, 1964.
———. *Paul: Apostle of the Heart Set Free*. Exeter: Paternoster, 1977.
Bucaklişi, I., et al. *Büyük Lazca Sözlük—Didi Lazuri Nenapuna*. Istanbul: Çiviyazıları, 2007.
Butzer, K. W. *Early Hydraulic Civilization in Egypt*. Chicago: University of Chicago Press, 1976.
Cansdale, G. *Animals of Bible Lands*. Exeter: Paternoster, 1970.
Chadwick, J. *Documents in Mycenaean Greek*. 2nd ed. Cambridge: Cambridge University Press, 1973.
Clark, W. E. "The Sandalwood and Peacocks of Ophir." *AJSL* 36 (1920) 103–19.
Cogan, M., and H. Tadmor. *2 Kings*. Anchor Bible Series. New York: Doubleday, 1988.
Cohen, H. R. *Biblical Hapax Legomena*. Missoula, MT: Scholars, 1978.
Collon, D. "Musik." In *RLA*, 8:488–91.
———. *Near Eastern Seals*. London: Trustees of the British Museum, 1990.
Cowley, A. E. *Aramaic Papyri of the 5th Century BC*. Oxford: Oxford University Press, 1923.
———. *Gesenius's Hebrew Grammar*. Oxford: Clarendon, 1910.
Craigie, P. C. *Psalms 1–50*. Word Bible Commentary Series. Waco, TX: Word, 1983.
Culcian, W. "Phoenicia and Phoenician Colonization." In *CAH*, 3/2:461–546.
Da Riva, R. "Nebuchadnezzar II's Prism (EŞ 7834): A New Edition." *ZfA* 103 (2013) 196–229.
Davies, G. I., et al. *Ancient Hebrew Inscriptions*. Cambridge: Cambridge University Press, 1991.
Deissmann, A. *Light from the East*. London: Hodder & Stoughton, 1911.
Dever, W. G. "Archaeology, Syro-Palestinian and Biblical." In *ABD*, 1:354–67.
Diakonoff, I. M. "The Naval Power and Trade of Tyre." *IEJ* 42 (1992) 168–93.
Diakonoff, I. M., and S. M. Kashkai. *Geographical Names according to Urartian Texts*. Wiesbaden: Reichert, 1981.
Dietrich, M., and O. Loretz. "Ug. bṣqlʿrgz und He. bṣqlnw (II Reg 4,22), 'gwz." *UF* 18 (1986) 115–18.
Driver, G. R. *Aramaic Documents of the Fifth Century BC*. Oxford: Clarendon, 1954.
Dzierzykray-Rogalski, T. "Paleopathology of the Ptolemaic Inhabitants of the Dakhleh Oasis (Egypt)." *JHE* 9 (1980) 71–74.
Ellenbogen, M. *Foreign Words in the Old Testament*. London: Luzac, 1962.
Engelmann, H., et al. *Die Inschriften von Ephesos*. Vol. 3. Bonn: Habelt, 1980.
Epstein, I. *The Babylonian Talmud, Seder Meʿod* 6. London: Socino, 1933.
Erman, A., and H. Grapow, eds. *Wörterbuch der Aegyptischen Sprache*. Vol. 5. Leipzig: Akademie, 1955.

Ertem, H. *Boğazköy metinlerine göre Hititler devri Anadolu'sunun Florası*. Ankara: Türk Tarih Kurumu, 1987.

Finet, A. *Le Code du Hammurapi*. Paris: Cerf, 1973.

Firmage, E. "Zoology." In *ABD*, 6:1109–67.

Forrer, E. *Die Provinzeinteilung des assyrischen Reiches*. Leipzig: Hinrichs, 1920.

Foster, B. J. "Gilgamesh." In *CoS*, 1:458–60.

Frye, R. N. *The Heritage of Persia*. London: Weidenfeld & Nicolson, 1962.

Gamkrelidze, T. V., and V. V. Ivanov. *Indo-European and the Indo-Europeans*. Vol. 1. Berlin: Mouton de Gruyter, 1995.

George, A. *The Epic of Gilgamesh*. London: Penguin, 2000.

Gordon, C. H. *Ugaritic Textbook*. Vol. 2. Rome: Pontifical Bible Institute, 1965.

———. *Ugaritic Textbook*. Vol. 3. Rome: Pontifical Bible Institute, 1965.

———. "The Wine-Dark Sea." *JNES* 37 (1978) 51–52.

Gray, G. B. *Isaiah*. International Critical Commentary Series. Edinburgh: T. & T. Clark, 1928.

Grayson, A. K. "Assyria: Sennacherib and Esarhaddon." In *CAH*, 3/2:103–41.

———. *Assyrian and Babylonian Chronicles*. Texts from Cuneiform Sources 5. Locust Valley, NY: Augustin, 1975.

———. *Assyrian Rulers of the Early First Millennium*. Vol. 1. Toronto: University of Toronto Press, 1991.

———. *Assyrian Rulers of the Early First Millennium*. Vol. 2. Toronto: University of Toronto Press, 1996.

Grenfell, B. P., and A. S. Hunt. *New Classical Fragments and Other Greek and Latin Papyri*. Vol. 2. Oxford: Clarendon, 1897.

———. *The Oxyrhynchus Papyri*. Vol. 2. London: Egypt Exploration Fund, 1899.

———. *The Oxyrhynchus Papyri*. Vol. 3. London: Egypt Exploration Fund, 1903.

Griesshammer, R. "Apis." In *BEAW*, 1:841–42.

Griffith, F. L. "The Teaching of Amenophis the Son of Kanakht." *JEA* 12 (1926) 191–231.

Habel, N. C. *Job*. Old Testament Library Series. London: SCM, 1985.

Hall, A. R., et al. *A History of Technology*. Vol. 2. Oxford: Clarendon, 1956.

Harell, J. E., et al. "Hebrew Gemstones in the Old Testament: A Lexical, Geological and Archaeological Analysis." *BBR* 27 (2017) 1–52.

Harris, J. R. *Lexicographical Studies in Ancient Egyptian Minerals*. Berlin: Akademie, 1961.

Hauser, S. R. "Archaeological Methods and Theories." In *BEAW Classical Tradition*, 1:216–32.

Heide, M. "The Domestication of the Camel." *UF* 42 (2011) 331–84.

Heidel, A. *The Gilgamesh Epic and Old Testament Parallels*. Chicago: University of Chicago Press, 1946.

Hepper, F. N. *Encyclopaedia of Bible Plants*. Grand Rapids: Baker, 1992.

———. "Trees." In *IllBD*, 1585–93.

Hoffmeier, J. K. *Israel in Egypt*. New York: New York University Press, 1997.

Holladay, W. L. *A Concise Hebrew and English Lexicon of the Old Testament.* Leiden: Brill, 1988.
Hope, E. R. *All Creatures Great and Small: Living Things in the Bible.* New York: United Bible Societies, 2005.
Hulse, E. V. "The Nature of Biblical 'Leprosy' and the Use of Alternative Medical Terms in Modern Translations of the Bible." *PEQ* 107 (1975) 87–105.
Hünemörder, C. "Apricot." In *BEAW*, 1:910.
———. "Haematite." In *BEAW*, 5:1090.
———. "Precious Stones." In *BEAW*, 11:795–96.
———. "Terebinth." In *BEAW*, 14:274–75.
Hunt, A. S. *The Oxyrhynchus Papyri.* Vol. 7. London: Egypt Exploration Fund, 1910.
———. *The Oxyrhynchus Papyri.* Vol. 17. London: Egypt Exploration Society, 1927.
Ikeda, Y. "Solomon's Trade in Horses and Chariots." In *Studies in the Period of David and Solomon and Other Essays*, edited by T. Ishida, 215–38. Winona Lake, IN: Eisenbrauns, 1982.
Jacob, I., and W. Jacob. "Flora." In *ABD*, 2:803–17.
Jacoby, F. *Die Fragmente der griechischen Historiker* 3C. Leiden: Brill, 1958.
Jastrow, M. A. *Dictionary of the Targumim, the Talmud Babli and Yerushalmi, and the Midrashic Literature.* New York: Pardes, 1950.
Jones, I. H. "Musical Instruments of the Bible, Part 1." *TBT* 37 (1986) 101–16.
Kaiser, W. C. "Exodus." In *EBC*, 2:287–497.
Kent, J. H. *Corinth* 8/3 *The Inscriptions 1926–1950.* Princeton: American School of Classical Studies at Athens, 1966.
Kenyon, F. G. *The Bible and Archaeology.* London: Harrap, 1940.
———. *Greek Papyri in the British Museum.* Vol. 1. London: Trustees of the British Museum, 1893.
———. *Greek Papyri in the British Museum.* Vol. 2. London: Trustees of the British Museum, 1898.
Kilmer, A. D. "Leier." In *RLA*, 6:571–82.
Kitchen, K. A. *Ancient Orient and the Old Testament.* Downers Grove: InterVarsity, 1966.
———. "Cush." In *IllBD*, 349–50.
———. "Food." In *IllBD*, 513–17.
———. "Punt." In *LÄ*, 5:1198–201.
———. "Regnal and Genealogical Data of Ancient Egypt." In *The Synchronisation of Civilisations in the Eastern Mediterranean in the Second Millennium BC*, edited by M. Bietak, 39–51. Vienna: Österreichischen Akademie der Wissenschaften, 2000.
Kitchen, K. A., and P. J. N. Lawrence. *Treaty, Law and Covenant in the Ancient Near East.* Vol. 1. Wiesbaden: Harrassowitz, 2012.
Kitchen, K. A., and T. C. Mitchell. "Chronology Old Testament." In *IllBD*, 268–77.
Köroğlu, K., and S. F. Adalı. *The Assyrians, Kingdom of the God Aššur from Tigris to Taurus.* Istanbul: Yapı Kredi Sanat Yayıncılık, 2018.

Konen, H. "Shipwrecks." In *BEAW*, 13:392–403.
Koops, R. *Each According to Its Kind: Plants and Trees in the Bible*." New York: United Bible Societies, 2012.
Kuhrt, A. *The Persian Empire—A Corpus of Sources from the Achaemenid Period*. London: Routledge, 2007.
Külzer, A. "Thera." In *BEAW*, 14:529–32.
Lambdin, T. O. "Egyptian Loan Words in the Old Testament." *JAOS* 73 (1952) 145–55.
Lane, E. W. *An Arabic-English Lexicon*. London: Williams & Norgate, 1863.
Lang, D. M. *Armenia Cradle of Civilisation*. 3rd ed. London: Allen & Unwin, 1970.
Lawrence, P. J. N. "Adam, Linnaeus and Lexicography." *TBT* 68 (2017) 142–47.
———. "Anatolia in the Old Testament." *Buried History* 36 (2000) 33–36.
———. "Bᵉrôš—A Study in Translational Inconsistency." *TBT* 55 (2004) 102–7.
———. *The Books of Moses Revisited*. Eugene, OR: Wipf & Stock, 2011.
———. "Elephants in the Bible." *Artifax* 31.2 (2016) 13–15.
———. *The Lion Atlas of Bible History*. Oxford: Lion Hudson, 2006.
———. "Making Some Sense of Babel and Afterwards." *JoC* 32 (2018) 110–14.
———. "Peacocks or Baboons." *TBT* 44 (1993) 348–49.
———. "Understanding Solomon's Wheeled Stands." *Yearbook on the Science of Bible Translation—14th Bible Translation Forum* (2018) 75–82.
———. "Uzziah—Inventor of the Catapult? A Note on 2Chr.26:15a." *Yearbook on the Science of Bible Translation—13th Bible Translation Forum* (2017) 119–23.
———. "Who Wrote Daniel?"*Artifax* 29.1 (2014) 16–21. Reprinted in *Bible and Spade* 28.1 (2015) 4–11.
Lawrence, P. J. N., and P. Schmidt, "Měkōnôt, Models and Mathematics." *TBT* 66 (2015) 61–72.
Lichtheim, M. "Instruction of Amenemope." In *CoS*, 1:115–22.
Lidzbarski, M. *Handbuch der Nordsemitischen Epigrafik*. Hildesheim, Germany: Olms, 1962.
Lobel, E., and C. H. Roberts. *The Oxyrhynchus Papyri*. Vol. 22. London: Egypt Exploration Society, 1954.
Lohwasser, A. "Meroe." In *BEAW*, 8:717–18.
Longman, T. "The Autobiography of Idrimi." In *CoS*, 1:479–80.
Loon, M. N. van. *Urartian Art*. Istanbul: Netherlands Historical Institute, 1966.
Luckenbill, D. D. *Ancient Records of Assyria and Babylonia*. Vol. 1. Chicago: University of Chicago Press, 1926.
———. *Ancient Records of Assyria and Babylonia*. Vol. 2. Chicago: University of Chicago Press, 1927.
Mallet, J., and V. Matoiän. "Commentaire des photos du chantier, le mobilier." *RSO* 14 (2001) 147–82.
Mallowan, M. E. L. *Nimrud and Its Remains*. Vol. 1. London: Collins, 1966.
Maniche, L. *An Ancient Egyptian Herbal*. London: British Museum, 1989.
Mann, C. S. *Matthew*. Anchor Bible Series 26. New York: Doubleday, 1971.

Marshall, I. H. “Jewels and Precious Stones.” In *IllBD*, 781–88.
Mattingly, G. L. “Ulu Burun.” In *DANE*, 306–7.
McCarter, P. K. “Gezer Calendar.” In *CoS*, 2:22.
McGrath, A. *In the Beginning*. London: Hodder & Stoughton, 2001.
Meek, T. J. “The Code of Hammurabi.” In *ANET*, 163–80.
Meiggs, R. *Trees and Timber in the Ancient Mediterranean World*. Oxford: Clarendon, 1982.
Mellaart, J. *Çatal Hüyuk: A Neolithic Town in Anatolia*. London: Thames & Hudson, 1967.
Michel, C., and P. Garelli. *Tablettes paleo-Assyriennes de Kültepe*. Istanbul: Bosphorus, 1997.
Millard, A. R. “The Babylonian Chronicle.” In *CoS*, 1:467–68.
———. “King Og's Bed.” In *JSOT* Supplement Series 67, 481–92.
———. *Reading and Writing in the Time of Jesus*. New York: New York University Press.
———. “What Has No Taste?” *UF* 1(1969) 210.
Mitchell, T. C. *The Bible in the British Museum—Interpreting the Evidence*. London: British Museum, 1988.
———. “Music in the Old Testament Reconsidered.” *PEQ* 124 (1992) 124–43.
Montagu, J. *Musical Instruments of the Bible*. Lanham: Scarecrow, 2002.
Moran, W. L. *The Amarna Letters*. Baltimore: Johns Hopkins University Press, 1992.
Morkot, R. G. “Ethiopia.” In *OCD*, 558.
Muchiki, Y. *Egyptian Proper Names and Loanwords in North West Semitic*. Atlanta: Society of Biblical Literature, 1999.
Murray, O. “The Ionian Revolt.” In *CAH*, 4:461–90.
Neeley, P. “Musical Instruments, Translating Biblical Names For.” In *GBT*, 616–17.
Norwich, J. J. *Byzantium—The Early Centuries*. London: Penguin, 1990.
Olmstead, A. T. *History of the Persian Empire*. Chicago: University of Chicago Press, 1948.
Oppenheim, A. L. *Ancient Mesopotamia*. Chicago: University of Chicago Press, 1964.
———. “Babylonian and Assyrian Historical Texts.” In *ANET*, 265–317.
Pardee, D. “The 'Aqhitu Legend.” In *CoS*, 1:343–56.
Parpola, S. *The Correspondence of Sargon II*. Part 1. State Archives of Assyria 1. Helsinki: Helsinki University Press, 1987.
Parpola, S. *The Prosopography of the Neo-Assyrian Empire* 1/1. Edited by Karen Radner. Helsinki: Helsinki University Press, 1988.
Payne, M. R. *Urartu Çiviyazılı Belgeler Kataloğu*. Istanbul: Arkeoloji ve Sanat Yayınları, 2006.
Pekridou-Gorecki, A. “Silk.” In *BEAW*, 13:462–64.
Pereltsvaig, A., and M. W. Lewis. *The Indo-European Controversy*. Cambridge: Cambridge University Press, 2015.
Philip, G. “Glass.” In *DANE*, 129–30.

Picken, L. *Folk Musical Instruments of Turkey*. Oxford: Oxford University Press, 1975.
Polhill, J. B. *Acts*. New American Commentary Series. Nashville: Broadman, 1992.
Postgate, J. N., and F. N. Hepper. "Terebinthe." In *RLA*, 13:594–95.
Prag, K. "The Excavations at Tell Iktanu 1989 and 1990." *Syria* 70 (1983) 269–71.
Pring, J. T . *The Oxford Dictionary of Modern Greek*. Oxford: Clarendon, 1982.
Pritchard, J. B. *The Ancient Near East in Pictures Relating to the Old Testament*. Princeton: Princeton University Press, 1954.
Rabin, C. "Hittite Words in Hebrew." *Orientalia* 32 (1963) 113–39.
Redhouse, J. *Türkçe-İngilizce Sözlüğü*. Istanbul: Redhouse, 1890.
Renger, J. "Ophir." In *BEAW*, 10:153–54.
Richardson, M. E. J. *Hammurabi's Laws*. Sheffield: Sheffield Academic, 2000.
Rimmer, J. *Ancient Musical Instruments of Western Asia*. London: Trustees of the British Museum, 1969.
Roth, M. "The Laws of Hammurabi." In *CoS*, 2:335–58.
Rowton, M. B. "Chronology." In *CAH*, 1:173–247.
Schneider, H. "Purple." In *BEAW*, 12:232–33.
Scholz, W. "Scripture." In *GBT*, 733–36.
Selms, A. van. "The Etymology of yayin 'Wine.'" *JNWSL* 3 (1974) 76–84.
Simpson, W. K. *The Literature of Ancient Egypt*. New Haven: Yale University Press, 1972.
Smelik, K. A. D. "The Inscriptions of King Mesha." In *CoS*, 2:137–38.
Smith, S. *The Statue of Idri-mi*. London: British Institute of Archaeology at Ankara, 1949.
Speiser, E. A. "Assyrian Myths and Epics." In *ANET*, 60–119.
Star, I. "Queries to the Sun God." State Archives of Assyria 4. Helsinki: Helsinki University Press, 1990.
Starke, F. "Asia Minor." In *BEAW*, 2:110–29.
Stauder, W. "Harfe." In *RLA*, 4:114–20.
Stradling, D. G., and K. A. Kitchen. "Music and Musical Instruments." In *IllBD*, 1031–40.
Streck, M. P. "Terebinthe." In *RLA*, 13:595–96.
Stohl, M. *On Trees, Mountains and Millstones in the Ancient Near East*. Leiden: Brill, 1979.
Sulimirski, T., and T. Taylor. "The Scythians." In *CAH*, 3/2:547–90.
Thomas, I. D. E., ed. *A Puritan Golden Treasury*. Edinburgh: Banner of Truth, 1997.
Thompson, R. C. *A Dictionary of Assyrian Botany*. London: British Academy, 1949.
Toy, C. H. *Proverbs*. International Critical Commentary Series. Edinburgh: T. & T. Clark, 1899.
Tristam, H. B. *Natural History of the Bible*. London: Clay, 1867.
Unger, E. *Babylon die Heilige Stadt nach der Beschreibung der Babylonier*. Berlin: de Gruyter, 1931.

Vermes, G. "Bible and Midrash: Early Old Testament Exegesis." In *CHB*, 1:199–231.

Ward, C., and C. Zazzaro. "Evidence for Pharaonic Seagoing Ships at Mersi/ Wadi Gawasis, Egypt." *IJNA* 39 (2009) 27–43.

Welten, P. *Geschichte und Geschichtsdarstellung in den Chronikbüchern*. Neukirchen-Vluyn: Neukirchener, 1973.

Wendorf, F., et al. "Egyptian Prehistory: Some New Concepts." *Science* 169 (1970) 1161–71.

Wilkinson, A. *The Garden in Ancient Egypt*. London: Rubicon, 1998.

Williamson, H. G. M. *Chronicles*. New Century Bible Series. London: Marshall, Morgan & Scott, 1982.

Wilson, J. A. "Proverbs and Precepts." In *ANET*, 412–25.

Wiseman, D. J. *The Alalakh Tablets*. London: British Institute of Archaeology at Ankara, 1953.

Wissmann, H. von. "Ophir." In *PRCAS*, 12:969–80.

Yamada, S. "The City of Togarma in Neo-Assyrian Sources." *AF* 33 (2006) 223–35.

Yamauchi, E. *The Stones and Scriptures*. London: InterVarsity, 1973.

Younger, K. L. "The Black Obelisk." In *CoS*, 2:269–70.

———. "The Siloam Tunnel Inscription." In *CoS*, 2:145–46.

Zaminer, F. "Musical Instruments." In *BEAW*, 9:346–49.

Zias, J. "New Evidence for the History of Leprosy in the Ancient Near East: An Overview." In *The Past and Present of Leprosy*, edited by C. A. Roberts et al., 259–68. *BAR* International Series 1054. Oxford: British Archaeological Reports, 2002.

Zohary, D., et al. *Domestication of Plants in the Old World*. 4th ed. Oxford: Oxford University Press, 2012.

Zohary, M. *Plants of the Bible*. Cambridge: Cambridge University Press, 1982.

Ancient Document Index

ANCIENT NEAR EASTERN DOCUMENTS

Akkadian

Alalakh tablet, 283b rev. 4; 275 rev. 3, 9, 16n6

Babylonian Chronicle 3, 66–68, 19n25

Esarhaddon, inscriptions, §21, 18; 51 episode 8, 3.43–46, 84n12
Esarhaddon, inscriptions, §66.23–24, 84n12
Esarhaddon, Query to Sun-god, §20, rev. 5–7, 86n22
Esarhaddon, Query to Sun-god, §35, obv.4; §66, obv.5; §71 rev.3′, 86n20

Idrimi, statue from Alalakh, 23, 37, 17n8

Nebuchadnezzar, prism 7834, 4.22, 21n29

Sargon II, correspondence, §30, obv.6′; §31, obv.9; 32 §32 obv.12, 84n6
Shalmaneser I, inscription, line 40, 83n2
Shalmaneser III, Black Obelisk, 105, 121, 85nn15–16.
Shalmaneser III, statue from Calah, 187′, 87n30
Suppiluliuma I, treaty of with Shattiwaza of Mitanni, 13, 20, 22, 87n27

Tiglath-pileser I, *Annals,* 6.62–63, 86n18
Tiglath-pileser I, *Annals,* 6.70, 72, 68n26

Aramaic

Sardis inscription of Artaxerxes (III ?), 92n57
Sefire Treaty 3, 4, 80n4

Egyptian

Instruction of Amenemope, 27.7, 18

Hebrew

Gezer Calendar, 3, 53n113

Lachish Letter, 4.10, 20

Tell Qasile inscription, 90n45

Ugaritic

2 Aqhat 6.36b–37a, 19n21

OLD TESTAMENT

Gen 2:13 88
Gen 4:21 27
Gen 8:4 83
Gen 9:20–21 46
Gen 10:2 83–85
Gen 10:3 86–87
Gen 10:4 88
Gen 10:6 88
Gen 10:14 89
Gen 10:26–29 89
Gen 25:34 41
Gen 30:37 48
Gen 31:27 31
Gen 37:25 56
Gen 40:9 45
Gen 41:2 57
Gen 41:42 53
Gen 43:11 48
Gen 47:31 24

Exod 5:3 76
Exod 9:31 53
Exod 9:32 42
Exod 10:19 93
Exod 16:31 43
Exod 24:10 1, 71
Exod 25:4 64
Exod 25:5 1, 50, 66
Exod 28:17 70–74, 70n2
Exod 28:18 71–73, 70n2
Exod 28:19 73–74, 70n2
Exod 28:20 74, 70n2
Exod 28:33 32, 46
Exod 28:35 32
Exod 30:34 66

Lev 11:13 62
Lev 11:15 62
Lev 11:16 59n2
Lev 11:17 62
Lev 11:18 59n2, 62
Lev 11:19 63
Lev 11:29–30 63
Lev 13:3–10 77
Lev 13:45 76
Lev 14:4 49
Lev 14:4 3 49
Lev 23:40 50

Num 10:2 33
Num 11:5 39–41
Num 19:6 49
Num 22:5 17
Num 23:22 59

Deut 2:23 89
Deut 3:11 24
Deut 29:17 44n42
Deut 33:17 59n6

Josh 17:16 24n14

Judg 9:15 49

1 Sam 10:5 27, 30
1 Sam 16:23 1, 27
1 Sam 18:6 34

2 Sam 6:5 28, 33–34
2 Sam 17:28 41

1 Kgs 4:23 61
1 Kgs 4:33 38, 58
1 Kgs 6:34 25n21
1 Kgs 7:27–37 12
1 Kgs 7:50 25
1 Kgs 10:11 51, 89
1 Kgs 10:12 28, 51
1 Kgs 10:18 ||2 Chr 9:17 67
1 Kgs 10:22 ||2 Chr 9:21 1, 60, 68, 88
1 Kgs 22:39 68

2 Kgs 4:42 19
2 Kgs 19:9 89
2 Kgs 19:13 ||Isa 37:13 92
2 Kgs 19:28 ||Isa 37:29 25

2 Kgs 23:29 19

1 Chr 4:21 54
1 Chr 13:8 34
1 Chr 15:16 28n14
1 Chr 15:20–21 28n15
1 Chr 15:28 28n14
1 Chr 16:5 28n14
1 Chr 25:6 28n14

2 Chr 2:7 51
2 Chr 5:12 28n14
2 Chr 9:10 51
2 Chr 9:17 ||1Kgs 10:18 67
2 Chr 9:21 ||1 Kgs 10:22 1, 60, 68, 88
2 Chr 26:1–14 22
2 Chr 29:25 28n14

Ezra 4:8—6:18 3n9
Ezra 7:12–26 3n9

Neh 12:27 28n14

Esth 1:1 91
Esth 1:6 2, 54

Job 6:6 1, 15–16
Job 28:17 75
Job 38:36 61–62

Ps 33:2 28
Ps 45:8 68
Ps 57:8 28n14
Ps 71:22 28n14
Ps 92:3 28
Ps 102:6 59n2
Ps 108:2 28n14
Ps 120:5 82, 86
Ps 137:1 50
Ps 144:9 28
Ps 149:3 26
Ps 150:5 28n14

Prov 22:20 17–18
Prov 25:11 47
Prov 26:23 18–19
Prov 30:17 62
Prov 30:31 61

Song 1:12 11
Song 4:13 11
Song 4:14 56
Song 5:14 67
Song 7:4 68

Isa 13:21 59n2
Isa 19:13 82n1
Isa 20:1 8n23
Isa 21:8 79–80
Isa 28:25 43–44
Isa 30:24 42
Isa 33:8 80
Isa 37:13 ||2 Kgs 19:13 92
Isa 37:29 ||2 Kgs 19:28 25
Isa 43:13 59n2
Isa 45:2 80
Isa 49:12 90
Isa 49:24 81
Isa 53:11 81

Jer 6:1 20
Jer 10:11 3n9
Jer 13:4 82n1
Jer 17:1 71n12
Jer 39:3 20–21
Jer 46:15 21
Jer 50:39 59n2

Ezek 3:9 71n12
Ezek 4:9 43
Ezek 16:10 2, 65
Ezek 16:10, 13 65
Ezek 27:6 68
Ezek 27:15 11, 52, 68
Ezek 28:13 70

Dan 2:4b—7:28 3n9
Dan 3:5 35–37

Hos 9:6 82n1

Amos 3:15 68
Amos 6:4 68

Obad 20 92

Jonah 4:6 55
Mic 1:8 59n2

Mic 1:16 62

Nah 3:6 82n1

Zech 7:12 71n12
Zech 9:16 70

NEW TESTAMENT

Matt 6:27 96–97
Matt 9:2 98
Matt 23:23 44
Matt 26:34 61
Matt 27:28 65
Matt 28:19–20 4

Mark 2:4 97
Mark 14:3 11
Mark 15:17 65

Luke 2:7 95n1
Luke 5:24 98
Luke 15:16 98
Luke 17:21 97
Luke 19:3 97

John 5:2 4n11
John 12:3 11
John 18:10 4n11
John 19:2 65

Acts 7:36 93
Acts 8:27 89
Acts 17:8 100–101
Acts 19:12 98
Acts 19:43 101
Acts 27:27 94
Acts 28:7 101

1 Cor 10:25 101
1 Cor 14:7 27n3

2 Cor 1:22 99

2 Tim 3:16–17 4
2 Tim 4:13 99

Heb 8:13 4n11
Heb 11:1 1, 95–96
Heb 11:21 24n11
Heb 11:29 93

1 Pet 5:4 100

Jude 14–15 3n8

Rev 5:8 27n3
Rev 8:13 11
Rev 18:12 52, 66
Rev 21:19–20 70

RABBINIC WRITINGS

Babylonian Talmud, *Sukkah*, 51b.25–26, 98n17

GRECO-ROMAN WRITINGS

Greek

Abydenus in Jacoby Die Fragmente der griechischen Historiker 3C, 401 §685, 5, 83n5
Aristotle, *History of Animals*, 547a.26–28, 64n44
Aristotle, *History of Animals*, 551b.16, 65n53

Letter of Aristeas, 9–11, 29–34, 173–86, 301–20, 5nn15–17

Herodotus, *Histories*, 1.103, 86n22
Herodotus, *Histories*, 2.94, 55
Herodotus, *Histories*, 3.106, 55
Herodotus, *Histories*, 3.112, 56n136
Homer, *Iliad*, 3.54, 35n77
Homer, *Iliad*, 8.221, 65n48
Homer, *Odyssey*, 1.59, 35n77
Homer, *Odyssey*, 8.248, 55n77
Homer, *Odyssey*, 11.14, 84n9
Homer, *Odyssey*, 19.225, 65n48

Josephus, *Against Apion*, 1.130, 83n4
Josephus, *Antiquities*, 13.68, 91n53
Josephus, *Jewish War*, 7.432, 91n53

Oxyrhynchus papyrus, 2.163, 96n2
Oxyrhynchus papyrus, 2.301, 99n20
Oxyrhynchus papyrus, 215.6.9, 100n27
Oxyrhynchus papyrus, 237.8.26, 96
Oxyrhynchus papyrus, 299.2–4, 99n20
Oxyrhynchus papyrus, 496.12, 97n7
Oxyrhynchus papyrus, 1020.5, 97n8
Oxyrhynchus papyrus, 2342.7–8, 97n10

Philo, *Life of Moses*, 2.37, 6n18
Plato, *Cratylus*, 405D, 36n84
Plato, *Laws*, 689D, 36n84
Plato, *Republic*, 531A, 36n84
Procopius, *History of the Wars*, 2.22.1–23.21, 76n3
Procopius, *History of the Wars*, 8.17.1–77, 66n57
Ptolemy, *Geography*, 3.15,44, 94n65

Latin

Caesar, *Gallic Wars*, 1.56; 6.30, 11n37
Codex Theodosianus, 10.20.18; 10.21.3, 65n47

Horace, *Satires*, 1.5.86; 2.6.42, 11n37

Manilius, *Astronomicon*, 4.296, 72

Pliny, *Natural History*, 13.92, 65n46

EARLY CHRISTIAN WRITINGS

Augustine, *Letter*, 71, 55n133

Subject Index

Aaron, Moses's brother, 32
Abydenus (2nd century AD), Greek historian, 83
Abydos, Egypt, 46
acacia, 50
Adriatic Sea, 94
African languages, 11, 73
agate, 74, 74n31
Ahab (873–53 BC), king of northern kingdom of Israel, 88
Akhenaten = Amenophis IV (1352–1336 BC), king of Egypt, 33
Akkadian (language), 16, 16n5, 73–74
Akzib, Israel, 31–32
Alaca Hüyük, Turkey, 36n82
'alāmôt musical term, 28n15
Aleppo, Syria, 17
Alexander the Great (336–23 BC), 6, 48, 77n5
Alexandria, Egypt, 5, 98n17
algum type of wood, 51–52
almond, 48
almug type of wood, 51–52
Amadāya, home of the Medes, 85
Amaw, Syria, 17
Amenemhat II (1917–1882 BC), king of Egypt, 71
Amenemope, Instruction of, 18
Amenemope, Onomasticon of, 93
Amenophis II (1428–1402 BC), king of Egypt, 45
Amenophis III (1392–1354 BC), king of Egypt, 44, 74
amethyst, 73
Ammisaduqa (1646–1626 BC), king of Babylon, 8n32
Anathoth, West Bank, 83n1
Apion, mentioned in a papyrus (late 1st century), friend of Horus, 99
Apis bull, 21
Aphroditopolis, Egypt, 88n38
apple, 47
apricot, 47
Aristotle (384–22 BC), Greek philosopher, 65
Apocrypha, 3, 3n8
Aqaba, Gulf of, 66n58
Aqhat, Epic of, 18
Aquila (ca. AD 140), Greek Bible translator, 6
Arabia, 52n105, 56, 89
Arabic version of Bible, 15
Arad, Israel, 42, 48
Aramaic (language), 3, 15n1
Aramaic, Bible portions in, 3n9
Ararat, Turkey, 46, 83
Archaeology, 2, 2n5
Ardys (after, 644 BC) king of Lydia, 84n13

Argishti (785/80–756 BC), king of Urartu, 87
Arimathea, 11n36
Aristeas, Letter of, 5
ark of the covenant, 34, 50
"Arkeology," 83n3
Armenia, 47, 87n25
Armenian version of the Bible, 7
Arsames, Persian satrap of Egypt, 92
Artaxerxes III (358–38 BC), king of Persia, 92n57
Ashurbanipal (668–30 BC), king of Assyria, 31n43, 84n13, 85
Ashur-uballit II (611–19 BC), king of Assyria, 19
Asia, Roman province of, 82
Asiarchēs,official in Roman province of Asia, 101
Aswan, Egypt, 73, 90, 90n49
Athens, Greece, 66
Attar-sumki (early, 8th century BC), king of Arpad, 80n4
Augustine (AD 354–430), church father, 55
Aurelius Asclepiades, makes a contract (AD 237) with Aurelius Theon, 99
Aurelius Theon, makes a contract (AD 237) with Aurelius Asclepiades, 99
Authorized (King James), Version, 7, 7n21, 15

baboon, 60
Babylon, throne room, 11
Babylonian (language), 8
Babylonian Chronicle, 19–20
Bacchus, Roman wine-god, 32n50
Badakshan, Afghanistan, 71
bagpipe, 36, 36n82
Balaam, false prophet, 17
Balak, king of Moab, 17
Ballah Lakes, Egypt, 93
Bar-Gayah (early, 8th century BC), king of KTK, 80n4
Barrakab, king of Sam'al, 29
Bartatua, king of the Ishkuzai = Protothyes, 86, 86n22
basalt, 7, 24
bed, 24, 68, 98
Behistun, Iran, 8, 91n50
bell, 32
Beni-Hasan, Egypt, 29, 53
Berossus (ca. 275 BC), Greek historian, 83
beryl, 73
Bethel, West Bank, 33
Beth-Hakkerem, 20
Beth-Shan, Israel, 33
Biainele, 83n2
Bible, 3, 3n6
Bible Translation, 4
Bismaya, Iraq, 29
Bitter Lakes, Egypt, 93
black cumin, 44
Black Obelisk of Shalmaneser III, 8, 60n10, 69, 85
blue purple, 64
Botta, Paul Émile (1802–1870), 7
broad bean, 41
Bubastis, Egypt, 61
bubonic plague, 76
Burgaz, Bulgaria, 32n50
Burnaburiash II (1359–1333 BC), king of Babylon, 71
Büyük Ağrı Dağı, Turkish name for Mount Ararat, 83

Calvin, John (1509–1564), 93
camel, domestication of, 58n1
Cape buffalo, 59
Caphtor = Crete, 89
Carchemish, Turkey-Syria, 17, 51
carob, 98
carrion vulture, 62
cassia, 39
castor oil plant, 55

Çatal Hüyük, Turkey, 53, 59
catapult, 23, 23n5
Cave of the Warrior, Jericho, West Bank, 53
cedar, 38, 49
Celsius, Olof (1670–756), 52n105
Celtic (language), 11
Chaeremon, mentioned in Oxyrhynchus papyrus (AD 186), father of Dionysia, 96
Champollion, Jean-François (1790–832), 7
Cheops (2593–2570 BC), king of Egypt, 49
Chester Beatty papyrus, 967, 88n38
chick pea, 42
chicken, 61
chief shepherd, 100
Chigi collection in the Vatican, 88n38
Ch'in dynasty in China (221–26 BC), 90
China, 47, 50, 66, 90
Chinese, 31n45
Cicero (106–43 BC), Roman leader and writer, 53n112
Cimmerians, 84, 86n24
cinnamon, 39
cistus, 56
Constantinople, Turkey, 76
Coptic versions of the Bible, 7
coriander, 43–44
Corinth, Greece, 101
Cos, Greece, 66
cotton, 54–55
cress, 67
Crete, Greece, 89, 94
crow, 62
cucumber, 39
cumin, 44
Cush = northern Sudan, 89

Dakhleh oasis, Egypt, 77
Daniel, dating of book, 3n10, 35n75
Darius I (520–486 BC), king of Persia, 8, 91n50
David (1010–970 BC), king of Israel, 34
Dead Sea Scrolls, 3n8, 9–10, 79–81
Debir, 11n36
Deir el-Bahri, Egypt, 49, 60
Delfshaven, Netherlands, 103
Demetrius of Phaleron, librarian of Alexandria, 5
Deutero-Isaiah, 90n47
diamond, 71, 71n12
Dibon, Jordan, 8
dill, 44–45
Diodorus Siculus (1st century BC), Greek historian, 23
Dionysia, mentioned in Oxyrhynchus papyrus (AD 186), daughter of Chaeremon, 96
door-socket, 25
Dravidian (language), 11n38, 60n8
dugong, 66
dulcimer, 36n81

eagle, 62
ebony, 11, 52
ed-Dhib, Muhammed, discoverer of the Dead Sea Scrolls, 9
Egyptian Hieroglyphic, 7
Elamite (language), 8
Elbistan, Turkey, 87
El Dorado, 88
Eleazar, Jewish High Priest under Ptolemy II, 5
elephant, 67–69
Elephantine, Egypt, 90
El Omari, Egypt, 53
emerald, 71–72
Emmaus, 11n36
emmer, 42
En-Gedi (Tel Goren), Israel, 30, 44
Enoch, Book of, 3n8
Epidaurus, Greece, 101n33

Ereğli, Turkey, 84
Ephesus, Turkey, 11, 101
Esarhaddon (680–669 BC), king of Assyria, 25, 84, 86
ESV 16n3
Ethiopia, 89
Ethiopic version of the Bible, 7
Euphrates, 17, 19–20, 82n1
exodus, the, 71n8

fattened birds, 61
Fayûm, Egypt, 99, 99n21
Fayûm A, prehistoric culture in Egypt, 53
feldspar, 73
fine linen, 53–54
fire-signals, 20
first installment, 99
flax, 53
flute, 30

Gamir, 84
Ganlidzha, Armenia, 87n25
garlic, 41
Georgian version of the Bible, 7
geese, 61–62
Gezer Calendar, 9, 53
Gezira, Sudan, 59
Gihon, river of paradise, 88
Gilead, Jordan, 56
Gilgamesh, Epic of, 8
Giza, Egypt, 49
glass, 75
glaze, 18–19, 75
Gog, 84
Gomer, 84
Gothic version of the Bible, 7
Grecian juniper, 52
greyhound, 61n15
Gualdaquivir, Spain, 88
Gürün, Turkey, 87
Guthios Pyrrhos, *Asiarchēs* from Hierapolis (early, 3rd century), 101
Gyges (d. 644 BC), king of Lydia, 84, 84n13

Hadhramaut, Yemen, 89
haematite, 72
halophytes, salt tolerating plants, 93
haloumi type of cheese, 16
Ham, son of Noah, 83
Hammurabi (1792–1750 BC), king of Babylon, 8, 8n32
Hansen, Gerhard (1841–1912), Norwegian scientist who named "Hansen's Disease," 77
harp, 27–30
Harran, Turkey, 19, 68
Hatshepsut (1479–1457 BC), queen of Egypt, 60
Havilah, Saudi Arabia, 89
Hawlan, Yemen-Saudi Arabia, 89
Hazarmaweth, Yemen, 89
ḥazzān synagogue attendant, 98n17
Heliopolis, Egypt, 91
Hereford, Nicholas (d. 1420), English Bible translator, 7n20
Herodotus (ca. 485–ca. 424 BC), Greek historian, 54–56, 56n136, 86n22
heron, 63
Hezekiah (715–686 BC), king of Judah, 11, 25
Hierapolis (Pamukkale), Turkey, 101
Himalayas, languages of, 11
Hindush = India, 91
hinge, 25, 25n18
Hiram, king of Tyre, 51, 89
Homer, Greek poet, 35n77, 65n48, 84n9
hook, 25
hoopoe, 63
Horace (65–68 BC), Roman writer, 11n37

Horus, mentioned in a papyrus (late 1st century), friend of Apion, 99
Hubushna = Ereğli, Turkey ?, 84
hummus, 42n26
Hurrian (language), 74
hyssop, 38, 38n1

ibis, 62
Idrimi (15th century BC), king of Alalakh, 17
India, 74, 77n5, 90–91, 91n50
iron, 24
Isaiah, Hebrew prophet, 25, 79–81, 90
Ishkuzai = Scythians, 86
Ishmaelites (or Midianites), 56
Ishme Dagan (18th century BC), king of Assyria, 48n77
Ishqigulu, land mentioned in Urartian inscriptions, 87
ivory, 29–31, 67–68

Jaazaniah (ca. 600 BC), owner of seal showing fighting rooster, 61
jacinth, 75n41
James I, king of England (1603–1635) (James VI of Scotland, 1567–1635), 7n21
Japheth, son of Noah, 83
jasper, 73n26, 74
Jehu (841–13 BC), king of northern kingdom of Israel, 8
jerboa, 63, 63n33
Jeremiah, Hebrew prophet, 20–21, 82n1
Jericho, West Bank, 41, 53
Jeroboam II (781–53 BC), king of northern kingdom of Israel, 68
Jerome (Sophronius Eusebius Hieronymus ca. AD 347–419), translator of Latin Bible, 6–7, 55
Jerusalem, 4n11, 5, 8, 11, 20, 22, 34, 61, 82n1, 91–92
Jesus, 3n6, 4, 65, 97
John, apostle, 4n11
Josephus (AD 37/38–ca. 100), Greek historian, 27, 83n4
Josiah (639–39 BC), king of Judah, 19
Judas tree, 64n41
Julius Caesar (100–144 BC), Roman leader and writer, 11n37
Julius Menkles Diophatos, *Asiarchēs* from Smyrna (AD 200–250), 101

Kadesh Barnea, Sinai, Egypt, 47
Kanesh (Kültepe), Turkey, 87
Kanlıca, Turkey, 87n25
Karahöyük, Turkey, 87
Karataş, Turkey, 77
Karnak, Egypt, 61
Kerameikos Necropolis, Athens, 66n55
Ketîb, an Aramaic term meaning "(the text as) written." 18n14
kettledrum, 37
Khartoum, Sudan, 73
Khirbet Qumran, West Bank, 9
Khnumhotep, Egyptian tomb owner, 29
Khorsabad, Iraq, 8
Kition, Cyprus, 88
Kittim = Kition, Cyprus, 88
Kültepe, Turkey, 87
Kuntillet ʿAjrud, Sinai, Egypt, 29

Lachish, Israel, 42, 48
Lachish Letters, 20
ladanum = rock rose, cistus, 56
Laḫiru, Iraq, 92
Lair = Laḫiru, Iraq, 92
La/ukarma, Turkey, 87
Lampōn, a mouse-catcher mentioned in a papyrus (late 1st century), 99

lapis lazuli, 1, 71
Lascaux, France, 59
Layard, Austen Henry, 8
Laz (language), 46, 47n65
Lechaion road, Corinth, Greece, 102
lentils, 41
Leontopolis, Egypt, 91
lizard, 63
Luther, Martin (1483–1546), 15, 93
Luwian (language), 87, 87n28
lyre, 27–29

Madai = Medes, 85
Maecia, wife of Quintus Cornelius Secundus of Corinth, 102
Magog, 84–85
Malchus, servant of Jewish High Priest, 4n11
mallow, 15–16
Malta, 101
Maʿmal, Saudi Arabia, 89
Manilius (1st century AD), Latin writer, 72
Marcheswan, month corresponding to October-November, 92n57
Mari, Syria, 48n77, 51n102, 67
Masada, Israel, 10
mat, 97
Mesopotamia, 16n5, 24
Masoretic Text, 79–81, 91
meat market, 101–2
Medes, 85
Megiddo, Israel, 12, 29–32
Memphis, Egypt (Heb. Moph/Noph), 21, 48n77, 82n1
Menodemus of Eritria, 5n14
Meritamon (1450–425 BC), queen of Egypt, 49
Meroë, Sudan, 89, 89n41
Mersa, Egypt, 50
Meshek = Mushku, Turkey, 82, 85–86
Midas, king of Phrygia = Mita of Mushku, 86
Mildenhall treasure, England, 32n50
Miletus, Turkey, 101
Mita of Mushku = Midas, 86
Mitanni, kingdom in eastern Turkey and northern Syria, 87, 87n27
Moabite Stone, 8
Mohenjo-Daro, Pakistan, 54
Mongolia, 86
monkey, 60
Moses, 6n19
Mostagedda, Egypt, 48n77
mouse, 63
mulberry, 66
Mumbai, India, 90
Mureybit, Syria, 41
Mushku, 85
muskmelon, 39
Mycenaean Greek, 44–45, 65n48

Nabopolassar (625–25 BC), king of Babylon, 20
Nahal Hever, West Bank, 10
nard, 11
Napoleon (1769–1821), 7
Nebo-Sarsekim (Nebu-šarussu-ukin), Babylonian official, 20–21, 21n30
Nebuchadnezzar (604–562 BC), king of Babylon, 20, 35
Necho (610–595 BC), king of Egypt, 19–20
Nergal-Sharezer of Samgar, Babylonian official, 20
Nimrud (Calah), Iraq, 8, 31, 43, 68–69, 87n30
Nineveh, Iraq, 23
Nippur, Iraq, 30, 48n77
NIV, 1n1
NKJV, 25n17, 80n3
Noah, 46, 83
NRSV, 16n3
Nubia, Sudan, 73, 89

oboe, 31
Oea, Tunisia, 55
Obadiah, Hebrew prophet, 92
Og, king of Bashan, 24
Old Church Slavonic version of the Bible, 3n8, 7
Old Latin version of the Bible, 6
Old Paphos, Cyprus, 24
Old Persian (language), 8, 91, 91n50
Omri (884–73 BC), king of northern kingdom of Israel, 8
Onias IV, Jewish high priest, 91
onion, 40
Onomasticon of Amenemope (ca. 1180–1100 BC), 93
onycha, 66–67
onyx, 74
Ophir, 51, 89–90
ostracon, 90n44
ostrich, 58, 59n2
owl, 59n2, 62
Oxyrhynchus, Egypt, 96–97

Pakistan, 54, 61, 91
Papyrus Ebers, 43
parchment, 99–100
pastry, 43n39
Paul, apostle, 4, 4n11, 98–99, 101
peacock, 60, 60n8
pelican, 59n2
Pentateuch, 6n19
Perath, 82n1
Pepi II (2287–2193 BC), king of Egypt, 40
peridot, 75n41
Peter, apostle, 4n11
Pethor, Syria, 17
Pharos, Egypt, 5
Philo of Alexandria, Jewish writer, 5
Philocrates, recipient of *Letter of Aristeas,* 5
Phrygia, Turkey, 86
pipe (musical instrument), 30–31
pistachio, 48
plectrum, 27, 27n3, 29n24
Pliny the elder (AD 23/24–79), Roman writer, 53n112
Phocaea (Foça), Turkey, 23
Pilgrim Fathers, 103
plane (tree), 49–50
Plato (428/7–348/7 BC), Greek philosopher, 36, 36n84
Po[blios] Aelios Martiales, *Asiarchēs* from Ephesus, 101
politarchēs, city official at Thessalonica, 101
pomegranate, 46
poplar, 50–51
Procopius (ca. AD 507–55), Greek historian, 66n57, 76n3
proto-Indo-European, 45
proto-Semitic, 45
prōtos, chief official of Malta, 101
Psalms, 3nn7–8, 28
psaltery, 36
Ptolemy (ca. AD 90–168), Greek geographer, 89–90, 94n65
Ptolemy II (285–46 BC), king of Egypt, 5, 5n14, 6, 93n63
Ptolemy V (203–181 BC), king of Egypt, 7
Publius, governor of Malta, 101
Punt, Sudan-Eritrea-Ethiopia, 60, 60n12
purple, 64–65, 65n46

Qerê, an Aramaic term meaning "(the text as) read," 52n106
Quintus Cornelius Secundus, builder of meat market at Corinth, 102
Qumran, West Bank, 9–10

Ramesses II (1279–1213 BC), king of Egypt, 47
Ramesses III (1184–1153 BC), king of Egypt, 59
Rashi (1040–1105), 93

Rashid, Egypt, 7
Rawlinson, Henry Creswicke (1810–895), 8
red hartebeest, 59
red jasper, 73
red purple, 64
red sandalwood, 52
red saunders, 52
Red Sea, 93
Reed Sea, 93
Rekhmire, Egyptian tomb owner, 69
Robinson, John (1576–1625), 103
rock rose, 56
rooster, 61
Rosetta, Egypt, 7
RSV, 15n3
Rusa I (719–14 BC), king of Urartu, 84
rushes, 93

Saadia Gaon (882–942), translator of Hebrew Bible into Arabic, 15
Saba, Yemen, 89
saffron, 56
Sājûr, Syria, 17
Sam'al (Zincirli), Turkey, 25, 29, 31
Samaria, West Bank, 68
Sanskrit (language), 52, 52n105, 54n126
Santorini (Thera), Greece, 56
sapphire, 71
Saqqara, Egypt, 21, 46
Sarapion, mentioned in Oxyrhynchus papyri (AD 127), husband of Thais, 97
sarcophagus, 24, 101
Sardinia, 88
Sardis, Turkey, 92
Sarepta, Lebanon, 64
Sargon (721–25 BC), king of Assyria, 8, 8n23, 84, 86
Scholastika baths at Ephesus, Turkey, 101
Scythians, 84, 84n12, 86n24
sea cow, 66
Sefire, Syria, 80n4
šemînît musical term, 28n15
Sennacherib (704–681 BC), king of Assyria, 25, 54, 83–84
Sepharad = Sardis, 92
Sepharvaim, 92
Septuagint, Greek translation of Old Testament (LXX), 3n7, 5–6, 21, 36, 55, 59, 67, 80–81, 88n38, 93
shadow of death, 17
shaduf, water-raising device, 24
Shalmaneser I (1273–1244 BC), king of Assyria, 83
Shalmaneser III (858–24 BC), king of Assyria, 8, 54, 60n10, 69, 85, 87
Shamash, Mesopotamian sun god, 86
Shattiwaza (14th century BC), king of Mitanni, 87
Sheba, Yemen, 89
Sheep Gate at Jerusalem, 4n11
Shem, son of Noah, 83, 89
Shiqmona, Israel, 64
Shubuhnu = Hubushna, 84n12
Shulgi (2094–2047 BC), king of Ur, 34n64
Sicily, 23, 94
Sidon, Lebanon, 66
silk, 65–66
Siloam Tunnel inscription, Jerusalem, 8
silver dross, 18
Sinim = Aswan ?, 90
Sinmagir, Iraq, 21
Sin-muballit (1812–1793 BC), king of Babylon, 40
sistrum, 33–34
Smith, George (1840–876), 8
Smyrna (İzmir), Turkey, 101

Solomon (970–930 BC), king of Israel, 38, 58, 89
Speedwell, The, 103
Sostratus of Cnidus (early 3rd century BC), architect of Pharos lighthouse, Alexandria, 5n16
Soupara, India, 89
Standard of Ur, 29
Sudan, 39n7, 59–60, 60n12, 89n39
Suez, Isthmus of, Egypt, 93, 93n63
Suppiluliuma I (14th century BC), king of the Hittites, 87, 87n27
Susa (Shushan), Iran, 8, 54
sweat cloth, 98
Syene, Egypt, 90, 90n49
Symmachus (late 2nd century AD), Greek Bible translator, 6, 91n52
Syracuse, Sicily, Italy, 23
Syriac version of the Bible, 7, 80–81

Tabālu = Tubal, 85
Tagari[immu] = Togarmah, 87
tambourine, 31–32
Tammuz, month corresponding to June-July, 19
Tap/blane = Tubal, 85n17
Tamil (language), 60n8
Targum, 15, 15n1
Tarsus, Turkey, 88
Tartessos, Spain, 88
Tegarama = Togarmah, 87
Tel Batash (Timnah), Israel, 29
Tel Dan, Israel, 34n1
Tel Goren (En-Gedi), Israel, 44n49
Tell Abu Hureyra, Syria, 41
Tell Atçana (Alalakh), Turkey, 16–17
Tell Basta (Bubastis), Egypt, 61
Tell Deir Alla, Jordan, 43
Tell el-Amarna, Egypt, 33
Tell el-Farʿah (South), Israel, 31
Tell el-Farʿah (North), Israel, 31
Tell en-Nasbeh, West Bank, 61
Tell Iktanu, Jordan, 48n77
Tell Qasile, Israel, 90
Thais, mentioned in Oxyrhynchus papyri (AD 127), wife of Serapion, 97
Thebes, Egypt (Heb. No-Amon), 9, 29, 69, 71, 82n1
Thebes, Greece, 71
Theodotion (late 2nd century AD), Greek Bible translator, 6, 36, 36n80, 88n38
thirty sayings, the, 17–18
Thoth, Egyptian god, 62
Tiglath-pileser I (1114–1076 BC), king of Assyria, 68, 85
Timbuktu, 86
Timna, Negev, Israel, 48
Timsah, Lake, Egypt, 93
TNIV, 1n1
Tod treasure, Egypt, 71
Togarmah, Turkey, 87
Toprakkale, Turkey, 65
treaty, 80n4, 87
trumpet, 33, 33n57
Tubal, Turkey, 85
turnip, 1, 16
turpentine, 48
turquoise, 72
Tushratta (14th century BC), king of Mitanni, 74
Tutankhamun (1361–1352 BC)'s tomb, 9, 24, 38, 40–44, 46, 48–49, 52–53, 73, 75
Tuthmosis III (1479–1425 BC), king of Egypt, 32, 59, 61
Tuthmosis IV (1401–1391 BC), king of Egypt, 30
Tyndale, William (ca. 1494–1536), English Bible translator, 7

Ugarit, Syria, 18–19, 34, 34n66, 51, 64
Ugaritic, 45n54

Uighurs, 31n45
Uluburun shipwreck, Turkey, 9, 33, 43–44, 46, 48, 52, 74–75
Unas (2392–2362 BC), king of Egypt, 40
unripe figs, 43n39
Ur, Royal Cemetery of (ca. 2500 BC), 9, 28, 47, 74
Urartu, kingdom in eastern Turkey, 46, 83–84
Uzbeks, 31n45
Uzziah (767–40 BC), king of Judah, 22–24

Valley of the Kings, Thebes, Egypt, 9
Van, Turkey, 65–66
Vardar Gate at Thessalonica, 101
Venus Tablet of Ammisaduqa, 8n32
vine, 45
vinegar, 42n26
Vulgate (Latin version of the Bible), 6, 7n20, 34n64, 55, 61n14, 62n21, 81, 93
vulture, 62

Wadi Baysh, Saudi Arabia, 89
Wadi Farah, West Bank, 83n1
Wadi Gawasis, Egypt, 50
Wadi Murabbaʿat, West Bank, 10
watermelon, 40
wheeled-stand, bronze, 12
white of an egg, 15–16
wild ox, 59
willow, 50–51
wine, 45–46, 97
Woolley, Leonard (1880–960), 9
wormwood, 44, 44n42
Wycliffe Bible, 7
Wycliffe, John (1324–1384), English Bible translator, 7n20

Xerxes (485–65 BC), king of Persia, 54

Yahdun Lim (ca. 1800 BC), king of Mari, 51n102
Yarkon, Israel, 90
Ybnn, 51
YHWH 8, 8n29

Zacchaeus, 97
Ziklag, Israel, 11n36, 32
zither, 27n3
Zoser (2691–2672 BC), king of Egypt, 46

Word Index (By Language)

AKKADIAN

adû treaty, 80n4
akbaru jerboa, 63
anpatu heron, 63
argamannu red purple, 64
āribu crow, 62
armannu apricot ?, 47
arqu yellow/green, 74n31

burallu a precious stone, 73
būṣu fine linen, 54
buṭnu terebinth, 48n75
buṭuttu pistachio, 48n75

duḫnu millet, 43n38

elemakku(m)/elemaggu(m) Cf. Heb. *almug*, 51
enšup/bu some kind of owl, 63
erēnu cedar, 49, 51n102

ḫašḫūru apple, 47n65
ḫilimetu a kind of vegetable, perhaps turnip, 16
ḫulālu a precious stone, 73
ḫulmiṭṭu snake/lizard, 63

(j)ašpû jasper, 74

kamūnu cumin, 44
karašu leek, 40
kunāšu emmer, 42, 42n31

ladin(n)u(m) ladanum, 56n136

pannigu cake, 43n39

qiššû melon, 39

rašāšu to melt, to be smelted, 88n33
rimu wild ox, 59

saḫlu/saḫlûtu cress, 67
sāmu red/brown, 74n31
sāmtu/sāmu onyx, 74
ṣalāmu to be dark, 17
ṣerru door pivot, 25n21
šebitu/sabītu type of harp, 36n79
šeḫlātu foodstuff/vegetable, 67
šubû agate ?, 74
šūmūm garlic, 41
šurminum cypress, 51n102

taskarinnum boxwood, 51n102
tašlamtu kind of lizard, 63

uqūpu monkey, 60n10

zakakatu glass, glaze, 75

ARABIC

dubb/dab lizard, 63n36
durrat millet, 43n36

gidda wormwood, 43

ḥallūm type of cheese, 16
ḥumus to be sour, 42n26

letem ladanum = rock rose, 56n136

nisr eagle, 62

raḥamu(n) carrion vulture, 62
sanṭur dulcimer, 36n81

timsah crocodile, 60n9
tuḥas dugong, 66

urjuwān purple, 64n41

wayn black grapes, 45

zil cymbal, 34n65

ARAMAIC

'dy treaty, 80n4

ḥallāmût juice of the mallow, 16

pesanṭērîn psaltery, harp, 36

qayterôs lyre, 35

sabka four-stringed harp, 36
supōnyā musical instrument, 36

ARMENIAN

zil cymbal, 34n65

CHINESE

ta-pu tambourine, 31n45

COPTIC

emsaḥ crocodile, 60n9

halom type of cheese, 16

DRAVIDIAN

tokei peacock, 60n8

EGYPTIAN

3ḥ(w) rushes, 57

'bw elephant, 68
bdw-k3 watermelon, 40

dḥwty ibis, 62

gf monkey, 60

hbny ebony, 52
ḥp Apis bull, 21
ḫnm.t red jasper, 73

kaka castor oil plant, 55
ky baboon, 60

mfk(3.t) green/blue turquoise, 72
mśy a kind of garment, 65n51

nšm.t feldspar, 73

p3ddt haematite, 72

qwqwpt/d hoopoe, 63

šnd.(t) acacia, 50
šś fine linen, 54

tpḥ apple, 47
thś leather, 66
twf(y) papyrus, 93

wnš.(t) wine, 45

GEORGIAN

ǧvino wine, 46

GREEK

Classical and Koiné

αδαμας *adamas* diamond, 72n13
Αιθιοψ *Aithiops* Ethiopian, 89
αλεκτωρ *alektōr* rooster, 61
αμεθυστος *amethustos* amethyst, 73n23
ανηθον *anēthon* dill, 44
αρραβων *arrabōn* first installment, 99
αρχαιολογια *archaiologia* Antiquarian law, ancient legends, history, 2
αρχιποιμην *archipoimēn* chief shepherd, 100

εντος *entos* within, with, 97

ἡλικια *hēlikia* stature, lifespan, 97

θεοπνευστος *theopneustos* God-breathed, 4n13
θυινος *thuinos* citron wood, 52

καταλυμα *kataluma* guest room, 95n1
καταπελτης *katapeltēs* war engine, 23n5
καταπελτικον *katapeltikon* catapult, 23
κερατια *keratia* pods, 98
κιθαρα *kithara* a kind of lyre or lute, 35
κιθαρις *kitharis* variant of the above, 35n77
κικι *kiki* castor oil plant, 55
κλινη *klinē* bed, 98
κλινιδιον *klinidion* little bed, 98
κοκκινος *kokkinos* scarlet, 65
κολοκυνθη *kolokunthē* round gourd, 55n131
κραβαττος *krabattos* mat, 98

λαδανον *ladanon* rock rose, 56, 56n136
λεπρα *lepra* "leprosy" skin-disease, 77

μακελλον *makellon* meat market, 101
μεμβρανα *membrana* parchment, 99
μονοκερως *monokerōs* rhinoceros, 59

ναρδος *nardos* nard, 11

ορχηστρια *orchēstria* dancing girls, 99

πανδοχειον *pandocheion* inn, 95n1
πελεκαν *pelekan* pelican, 59n2
πετροβολοι *petroboloi* engines for throwing stones, 23
πορφυρα *porphura* purple, 65
πορφυρους *porphurous* purple, 65

(ϝ)οινος (*w*)*oinos* wine, 45

ῥεδη *rhedē* carriage, 11, 11n37

σαμβυκη *sambukē* musical instrument, 36
σαπφειρος *sappheiros* sapphire, 71n5
σαπφιρυον *sapphiruon* sapphire, 71n5

σειστρον *seistron* sistrum, 33n58
σιρικος *sirikos* silk, 66
στακτη *stactē* oil of myrrh, 56n134
σουδαρια *soudaria* sweat-cloths, 98
συμφωνια *sumphōnia* concord, harmony, 36

τυμπανον *tumpanon* kettledrum, 37

ὑποστασις *hupostasis* title deed, 96

ψαλτηριον *psaltērion* psaltery, harp, 36

Modern

δαχτυλιδι αρραβωνα *dhachtilidhi arravona* engagement ring, 99, 99n24

κρεββατι *krevvati* bed, 98n11

Mycenaean

kumino cumin, 44

popureja purple, 65n48

wanakatero kingly, 65n48
wono wine, 45

HEBREW

Biblical

abaṭṭiaḥ watermelon, 40
'adāšāh lentils, 41
aḥlāmāh red jasper, 73
āḥû rushes, 57
'akbār mouse, 63
algum, 51–52
almug, 51–52
anāpāh heron, 63
'arābāh willow/poplar, 50–51
argāmān red purple, 64
'ārîṣ fierce, 81
aryēh lion, 79

barburîm abûsîm fattened birds, 61
bāreqet beryl, 71, 71n3, 73
bāṣāl onion, 40
berîr ḥallāmût white of an egg, 15
berôš evergreen/conifer, 28, 51, 51n99
beṣiqlōnô heads of new grain, 19
boṭnāh pistachio, 48
bûṣ fine linen, 54

deber plague, 76
dōḥan millet, 43
dûkîpat hoopoe, 63

'ēdîm vassal treaty, 80
'ērābôn pledge, 99n18
ereś bed, 24
erez cedar, 49
`ermôn plane (tree), 49

gad coriander, 43
gālîl socket, 25n21
gepen vine, 45

hab elephant, 68
hābenîm ebony, 11, 52
heres destruction, 91
ḥaḥ hook, 25
ḥālîl pipe, 30
ḥāmîṣ chick pea, 42
ḥāṣîr leek, 40
ḥaṣōṣerāh trumpet, 33
ḥeres sun, 91
ḥiššebōnôt inventions, 23
ḥōmēṣ vinegar, 42n26
ḥōmeṭ kind of lizard, 63

kammōn cumin, 44
karkōm saffron, 56
karpas cotton, 54
kinnôr lyre, 27, 27n3, 28, 28nn14–15
kussemet emmer, 42

la'anāh wormwood, 44n42
lešem feldspar, 73
lōṭ rock rose, cistus, 56
lûz almond, 48

maśēt fire-signal, 20
mekōnāh wheeled-stand, 12
mena'an'îm sistrum ?, 33
meṣiltayim cymbals, 34
mešî silk, 65
miṭṭāh bed, 24

nēbel harp, lyre, 27–28, 28nn14–15
nerd nard, 11
nešer eagle, vulture, 62
nōpek green/blue turquoise, 72

ōdem carnelian, 74
'ōrēb crow, 62

pa'amôn bell, 32
pannag millet, 43
pištāh flax, 53
piṭdāh haematite, 72, 75n41
pôl broad bean, 41
pōtôt (door)-socket, 25

qeṣaḥ black cumin, 44
qiššuāh muskmelon, 39
qiyqāyôn castor oil plant, 55
qōp monkey, 60

rāḥām carrion vulture, 62
reēm wild ox, 59
rimmôn pomegranate, 46
rōeh lookout, 80
sekwî rooster, 61

ṣāb lizard, 63n36
ṣalmāwet shadow of death, 17
ṣāra'at "leprosy" skin disease, 77
ṣelṣelîm cymbal, 34, 34n66
ṣîr hole for door pivot, 25

śôrāh millet, 43
šālîšîm sistrum ?, 34
šāmîr emery, 72n12
šāqēd almond, 48
šebô agate, 74
šeḥēlet onycha/a type of vegetable, 66
šelôšîm thirty, 18
šenhabbîm ivory, 68
šereṣ creeping thing, 63n33
šēš fine linen, 53–54
šilšôm excellent things, 18
šiṭṭîm acacia, 50
šōham onyx, 74
šûm garlic, 41

taḥaš sea cow/fine leather, 66
tappûaḥ apple, 47
teaššûr cypress ?, 51n101
tekēlet blue purple, 64
tinšemet kind of lizard, 63
tōp "tambourine", frame-drum, 31–32
tukkîm baboons, 60
ṭuḥôt ibis, 62
'ûgāb flute, 30

yam sûp sea of reed, 93, 93n63
yanšûp some kind of owl, 62
yašpēh jasper, 74
yayin wine, 45

zarzîr rooster, 61
zekôkît glass, 75

Modern

'ermôn chestnut, 49n87

pannag pastry, 43n39

qiyqāyôn castor oil, 55n132

sekwî rooster, 61n14

HITTITE

arg/kamman tribute, 64

kinirri(laš) lyre, 27n3

maššiya shawl, 65n51

punniki baked food, 43n39

wiyana wine, 45

zaḫḫeli cress, 67

LATIN

cithara lyre, 35n77
curcurbita gourd, 55n131
ebur ivory, 68n68

gallo rooster, 61n14

hedera ivy, 55

membrana parchment, 100

panicum millet, 43

reda/raeda wagon, 11n37

sudarium sweat cloth, 98

vinum wine, 45

LAZ

ğvini wine, 46

uşkuri apple, 47n65

PERSIAN (MODERN)

arğavān purple, 64n41

santir dulcimer, 36n81

SANSKRIT

karpâsa cotton, 54

pita yellow, 72

markata emerald, 72

nálada/narada nard, 11n38

sanipriya sapphire, 72

SUMERIAN

ḫašḫur apple, 47n65

GIŠ*sa.eš-dar* musical instrument, 34n64

TAMIL

tokai tail, 60n8

TURKISH

erguvan purple, Judas tree, 64n41

laden ladanum, rock rose, 56n136

santur dulcimer, 36n81

zil cymbal, 34n65

UGARITIC

almg Cf. Heb. *almug*, 51
argmn red purple, 64n40

bṣql corn stalk, 19

nšr eagle, 62

spsg glaze, 19
šḫlt a vegetable, 67

tišr cypress, 51n101

yn wine, 45

Index of Zoological and Botanical Names

Acacia nilotica, 50
Allium cepa, 40
Allium kurrat, 40
Allium sativum, 41
Amygdalus communis, 48
Anethum graveolens, 44
Armeniaca vulgaris, 47

Bombyx mori, 66
Bos primigenius, 59

Callitris quadrivalvis, 52
Cedrus libani, 49
Ceratonia siliqua, 98
Cercis siliquastrum, 64n41
Cicer arietinum, 42
Cistus creticus, 56
Cistus laurifolius, 56
Citrullus lanatus, 40, 40n11
Citrullus vulgaris, 40n11
Coriandrum sativum, 43
Crocus sativus, 56
Cucumis melo, 39
Cucumis sativus, 39
Cuminum cyminum, 44

Dalbergia melanoxylon, 52
Diceros bicornis, 60
Diospyros ebenum, 52n108
Dugong dugong, 66n58

Elephas maximus asurus, 69
Elephas maximus indicus, 69

Gossypium arboreum, 55n129
Gossypium herbaceum, 54
Gyps fulvus, 62

Helicore helicore, 66n58
Hyssopus officinalis, 38n1

Juniperus excelsa, 52

Lens culinaris, 41
Linum usitatissimum, 53
Loxodonta africana pharaoensis, 69

Malus pumila, 47
Malus sylvestris, 47
Murex brandaris, 64
Murex trunculus, 64

Nardostachys jatamansi, 11n38
Nigella sativa, 44

Origanum maru, 38n1
Origanum officinalis, 38n1
Origanum syriacum, 38n1

Pachypasa otus, 66
Panicum milaceum, 43n37
Papio cynocephalus, 60
Papio hamadryas, 60
Pimpinella anisa, 45
Pistacia palaestina, 48
Pistacia terebinthus, 48
Populus euphratica, 50
Platanus orientalis, 49
Pterocarpus santolinus, 52
Punica granatum, 46

Rhinoceros unicornis, 60
Ricinus communis, 55

Salix babylonica, 50
Struthio camelus, 59n2
Syncerus caffer, 59

Tetraclinis articulata, 52
Threskiornis aethiopica, 62

Upopa epops, 63

Vicia faba, 41
Vitis sylvestris, 45
Vitis vinifera, 45
Vultur percnopterus, 62

www.ingramcontent.com/pod-product-compliance
Lightning Source LLC
Chambersburg PA
CBHW070917180426
43192CB00038B/1738